# INDIAN COURT PAINTING

## 16TH–19TH CENTURY

# INDIAN COURT PAINTING

## 16TH–19TH CENTURY

S T E V E N  K O S S A K

The Metropolitan Museum of Art, New York

Distributed by Harry N. Abrams, Inc., New York

This catalogue is published in conjunction with the exhibition "Indian Court Painting: 16th–19th Century," held at The Metropolitan Museum of Art, New York, from March 25 to July 6, 1997.

The exhibition is made possible by the **Lita Annenberg Hazen Charitable Trust.**

This publication is made possible by the **Doris Duke Fund for Publications.**

Published by The Metropolitan Museum of Art, New York
John P. O'Neill, Editor in Chief
Barbara Burn, Executive Editor
Ruth Lurie Kozodoy, Editor
Bruce Campbell, Designer
Matthew Pimm, Production

Separations made by Professional Graphics, Inc., Rockford, Illinois
Typeset in Bembo and Post Antiqua
Printed and bound by Amilcare Pizzi S.p.A.-arte grafiche, Milan

LIBRARY OF CONGRESS CATALOGING-IN-PUBLICATION DATA

Kossak, Steven.
   Indian court painting, 16th-19th century / Steven
      Kossak.    p.    cm.
   Includes bibliographical references and index.
   ISBN 0-87099-782-3 (hc). — ISBN 0-87099-783-1
      (pbk. : alk. paper). — ISBN 0-8109-6508-9 (Abrams)
   1. Miniature painting, Indic — India — Exhibitions.
      1. Title.   ND1337.15K68   1997
   751.7'7'09540747471—dc21     96-53500   CIP

Jacket/cover illustration: Detail of *King Dasharatha and His Royal Retinue Proceed to Rama's Wedding*, ca. 1680–90, The Metropolitan Museum of Art, New York (cat. no. 42)

Frontispiece: The Mandi Master, *Maharaja Sidh Sen Receiving an Embassy*, ca. 1700–1710, The Metropolitan Museum of Art, New York (cat. no. 45)

# CONTENTS

Foreword      vii

Acknowledgments      ix

FOUR CENTURIES OF INDIAN PAINTING      3

CATALOGUE      25

Selected Bibliography      135

Lenders to the Exhibition      137

Index      138

Photograph Credits      142

# FOREWORD

Historical accident has placed at opposite ends of The Metropolitan Museum of Art its outstanding collection of Mughal painting, housed in the Islamic Art department, and its growing holdings of Hindu court painting, kept in the department of Asian Art. Indeed, it is common practice for these two artistic traditions to be treated separately. "Indian Court Painting: 16th–19th Century," mounted to honor the fiftieth anniversary of Indian independence, redresses that division, bringing these diverse aspects of Indian painting during its golden age into a single chronological continuum. Within this framework it has been illuminating to investigate the historical and aesthetic milieus in which the paintings were made and to explore stylistic connections between them.

To the ebullient images that emerged from an indigenous Rajput tradition, characterized by bold pattern, nonrealistic use of color, and a shallow space, the style of the Mughal invaders presented a complete antithesis. Mughal pictures were subtle and naturalistic, often giving the illusion of deep spatial recession. While Rajput arts concentrated on mythical subjects, Mughal paintings more often depicted historical events or court life. But as the Rajput principalities came under the sway of Mughal emperors during the late-sixteenth and seventeenth centuries, many of the princes founded painting ateliers, and in these the artistic approach and subject matter favored by their overlords were, to varying degrees, adopted. Within the larger cross-fertilization of Islamic and Hindu culture that ensued, each of these states developed its own distinctive vocabulary; even in the smaller courts, hybrid painting styles blossomed that were original and refined. This tendency reached its high point toward the end of the seventeenth century. Although the following century witnessed the decline of the Mughal dynasty and the reassertion of indigenous strains in many Rajput centers, the history of Indian court painting remains that of a perpetual artistic conversation.

Often Indian painting is thought of as a miniature tradition, but small-scale, finely wrought images are only one facet of court production. By the eighteenth century Rajput ateliers were increasingly making large pictures along with those of traditional size. In this catalogue the scale of the reproductions is roughly relative to the sizes of the works, so the reader can quickly apprehend these important differences in scale.

For this exhibition eighty-three exceptional pictures have been gathered, about a third of them generously lent by their owners, the rest drawn from the extensive collections of The Metropolitan Museum of Art. The core of our Mughal holdings consists of three important acquisitions. The first, a set of pages from a dispersed manuscript, was the gift of Alexander Smith Cochran in 1913. Paintings from Islamic India were often assembled in albums, and two notable albums have come to the Museum: one was a bequest from Theodore M. Davis in 1915 and the other was purchased, in part with support from The Kevorkian Foundation, in 1955. Individual works have been added over the years to round out and strengthen our Islamic Indian holdings, a process that continues.

Paintings from the Hindu courts of India have been acquired somewhat more haphazardly, beginning in 1918 with a purchase of seven works from the collection of the great Indian art historian Ananda Coomaraswamy and continuing through sporadic purchases and gifts. Until recently no consistent effort had been made to assemble a representative collection, but during the last few years the Museum has slowly been developing a core of exemplary Rajput and Pahari works. A number of them are published for the first time in this catalogue.

With their brilliance of color and line and their astonishing vitality, these images draw us into a rich world of splendor and fantasy. Their immediate appeal transcends all cultural boundaries.

Philippe de Montebello
*Director, The Metropolitan Museum of Art*

# ACKNOWLEDGMENTS

First, I would like to express my profound gratitude to the private collectors and institutions who generously lent paintings for this exhibition: Dr. Alvin O. Bellak, Ronnie and Walter Eisenberg, Howard Hodgkin, The Knellington Collection, The Kronos Collections, Helen Marden, the Philadelphia Museum of Art, the Arthur M. Sackler Museum of Harvard University Art Museums, the San Diego Museum of Art, Anita Spertus, Stuart Cary Welch, Doris Wiener, and those who lent anonymously.

Many people gave freely of their time and expertise to help me prepare this project. I have benefited from discussions on scholarly matters large and small with Terence McInerney, Christopher Noey, Rashmi Poddar, and Ellen Smart, and with Mimi Swietochowski and Daniel Walker of the Museum's Department of Islamic Art. My thanks for various kinds of help also go to Nancy Baxter, Pia Brancaccio, Rochelle Kessler, and Andrea Wolf. I am particularly grateful to Mahrukh Tarapor, without whose support the project could not have been realized.

The publication of this catalogue was professionally carried out by members of the Metropolitan Museum's Editorial Department. I thank John P. O'Neill and Barbara Burn, who provided support and valuable guidance. I am grateful to Ruth Kozodoy, who edited the book with élan and coordinated its progress throughout; Matthew Pimm, who skillfully managed its production; and Bruce Campbell, the creator of its handsome design. I also thank Jean Wagner, editor of the bibliography; Barry Girsh, who made the map; and Peter Rooney, who prepared the index.

Finally, much-appreciated support for mounting the exhibition came from Cynthia Hazen Polsky and the Lita Annenberg Hazen Charitable Trust. I am also grateful to the Doris Duke Fund for Publications, which helped make it possible to publish this catalogue.

S. K.

# INDIAN COURT PAINTING

## 16TH–19TH CENTURY

# FOUR CENTURIES OF INDIAN PAINTING

From the sixteenth through the nineteenth century, ateliers at the royal courts of North and Central India produced paintings on paper or cloth for the delectation of the rulers and their immediate circles. This was a period of diversity in virtually every realm, and Indian court painting is usually divided into four major traditions whose milieus are defined in terms of religion, polity, and geography: the Muslim kingdoms of the Mughals (centered in Delhi) and of the Deccani sultans (on the central plateau); and the Hindu Rajput kingdoms in Rajasthan (on the plains) and in the Punjab Hills. The history of each of these artistic traditions extends over several centuries and encompasses many small ateliers, all of which had their own evolving traditions. In this essay the intent is only to introduce some high points of this vast panorama and to explore ways in which the elements of its varied topography are joined.

Hindu and Muslim rulers were members not only of different religions but of distinct cultures, and the themes they chose to illustrate were initially quite unlike. For Muslims, called "the people of the book" because of their devotion to the Koran, reading and the sense of an evolving place in history were particularly important. Painted works produced in the Islamic courts had mostly temporal themes. There were books of history both contemporaneous and legendary, literary and poetic works, portraits of the rulers and their courtiers, vignettes of court life, and studies of natural history. Books were bound, and text and illustration were often accorded equal importance.

In contrast, Hinduism relied on the oral transmission of religious texts in which time was understood as cyclical and temporal matters were comparatively insignificant. Many of the texts had entered the realm of folklore. These popular religious stories were illustrated for the Hindu courts, along with writings in which specific aspects of human experience, especially love and heroism, were systemized by being broken down into numerous specific categories. These "systemizations" too have quasi-religious overtones, with the Hindu god Krishna and his consort, Radha, often taking the leading roles. Like the Muslim books, the manuscripts were made to be appreciated in a secular courtly context. But unlike the Muslim works, they were not bound,

*Opposite: Figure 1. Detail of Maharana Ari Singh with His Courtiers at the Jagniwas Water Palace, 1767. Mewar, Rajasthan. See cat. no. 72.*

3

and the text, which was familiar to the audience, was usually abbreviated and often relegated to the reverse side of the painted image. It served principally to identify the subject of the painting, when that was necessary.

Initially, distinctive Hindu and Muslim styles evolved in India, but over time the two interacted. In Indian painting the ebb and flow of patronage was one of the major mechanisms of this diffusion, and the Mughal imperial court played a particularly important role in the process. At crucial points during the seventeenth and eighteenth centuries, when royal patronage of the imperial atelier waned, its artists dispersed to smaller centers. In some cases the movement of artists is documented, but in others we must rely on stylistic analysis. The result of artists' peregrinations was a diversity of styles, not only between centers but also, sometimes, within them, and it was not unusual for a large atelier to have artists working in several different stylistic modes. Actual artistic innovation, however, tended to be sporadic and often short-lived: in many cases a tradition fluoresced briefly on the strength of enlightened patronage and the availability of inspired artists, only to revert to traditional modes of artistic expression.

Political factors also influenced the spread of styles. The Rajasthani kingdoms were brought within the Mughal orbit as feudatory states through treaties of various kinds, and the rajas became subjects of the emperor, ruling by his largess. They were obliged to support the emperor militarily and to attend his court. In certain cases the emperor partitioned an existing state, often to weaken its military might, or for some other reason created a new state through an imperial land grant. The Rajput warriors who became leaders of the new states acquired status and independence, but they also owed particular allegiance to the emperor and often were called upon to spend most of their time fighting or doing administrative work in a Mughal setting, away from their own courts. These feudal obligations fostered the adoption of Mughal culture in Rajasthan. (Some Rajput rulers were able to maintain a greater distance from the imperial court and so absorbed less of its influence.) Additionally, a continuing cultural interchange was established when a Rajasthani noblewoman married into the Mughal royal family. Royal women frequently commissioned paintings and thus played a central role in the cross-fertilization of styles.[1]

## EARLY PAINTING

Although there is little evidence that Hindu manuscripts were produced before the fifteenth century, Buddhist sculptures as early as the Gupta period (late third to fifth century) show deities holding manuscripts as attributes,

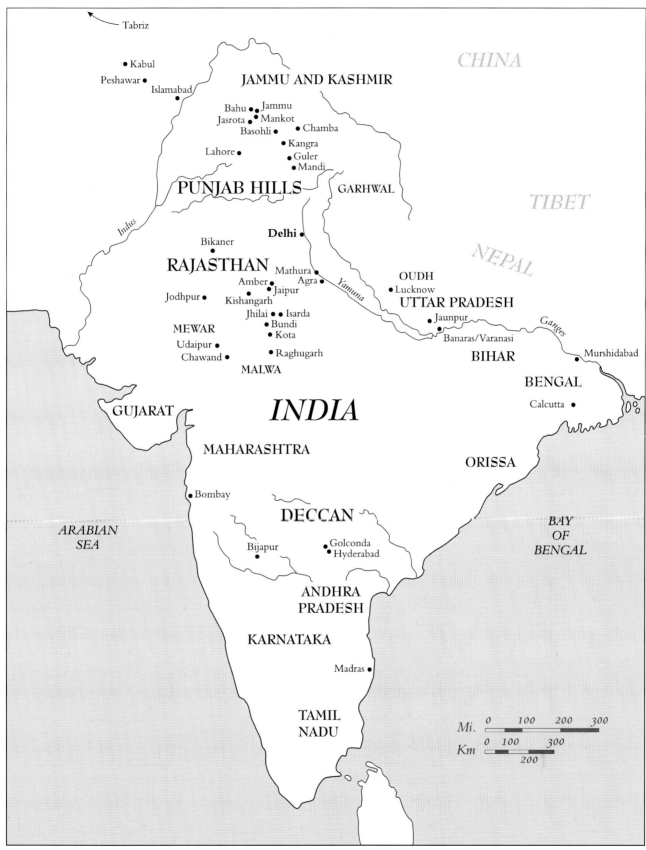

Figure 2. India, 16th–19th century, showing major centers of court painting in North and Central India

Figure 3. Page from a palm-leaf manuscript of the *Panca-vimsatisahasrika Prajnaparamita*, ca. 1090. Bengal school, Pala period. Ink and opaque water-color on palm leaf. The Metropolitan Museum of Art, New York, purchase, Weld Fund, 1952 (52.93.2)

indicating that in India the manuscript tradition is very old. The principal illustrated texts that survive from before the sixteenth century were made as religious donations or for religious use by the Buddhist and Jain communities. The vast majority of the Buddhist manuscripts date from the eleventh and twelfth centuries; by the thirteenth century Buddhism had largely been extinguished in North India.

For Buddhists the written word was considered a vessel of the transcendent as potent as sculptural representation, and manuscripts not only were regarded as sacred but were themselves objects of veneration. The palm leaves on which they were written dictated their long, narrow format (fig. 3). The leaves were enclosed between wooden boards whose inside surfaces were sometimes painted with rows of divinities or with episodes from a particular narrative, such as scenes from the life of the Buddha. Some of the palm-leaf pages carried small pictorial illuminations, but these were usually iconic rather than narrative and did not illustrate the text.

Contemporaneous manuscripts of the Jain community, whose religion originated in India in the sixth century B.C., also utilized palm leaves. By the last quarter of the fourteenth century, however, paper became the preferred support. The old elongated format, which had been necessitated by the narrow shape of the palm leaf, evolved into a more compact, rectangular shape that was later to prove well suited to larger illustrations and elaborate marginal designs. The Jain manuscripts contain stock images or small scenes illustrating the text, usually carried out in a restricted color scheme (see cat. no. 1). White, yellow, red, green, and blue-black, the fundamental colors in Indian art, form the basic palette of Jain painting as well as of the first Hindu court paintings.

The oldest extant illustrated Hindu texts are from the second half of the fifteenth century and relate to the Jain manuscript tradition. In the early sixteenth century a distinctive new style arose that appears in illustrations of both secular and popular-religious subjects. These works must have been produced for the rajas or other wealthy patrons of North India. Unlike the Jain and Buddhist manuscripts discussed earlier, in which illuminations are generally secondary to the text, here the pictorial representations are predominant. An abbreviated version of the text is relegated to the upper margin of an

6

illustrated page, and a more extended text fills the obverse. By now the page has become a classical rectangle in shape, enabling it easily to accommodate a full-page horizontal image. Clearly the function of the manuscript has changed: visual requirements have replaced literary ones, and the artist seeks to inspire rather than inform the imagination of the viewer (cat. nos. 2–6).

The reasons for this unheralded shift and the renaissance of painting accompanying it are unclear. The Hindu myths and epics forming the basis of the early illustrated texts had passed long before into the realm of popular culture. Nor are there any particular signs that inspiration for these manuscripts came from the influence of Indian Muslim kingdoms of the early sixteenth century. Despite those early Islamic kingdoms' great architectural legacy, what little survives of their books displays a rather provincial blend of Persian and Indian motifs. Although Muslim courts of the same period in Persia and Turkestan accorded their manuscript ateliers great prestige, either the enterprise was not of like importance to these early Indian Muslim courts or they simply could not attract trained artists of the highest caliber.

The indigenous Indian style has come to be known by the name of one of the earliest manuscripts of the group, the *Chaurapanchasika* (Fifty stanzas of secret love), a "systemization" of love that describes a poet's clandestine tryst with a princess on the eve of his execution. Many of this style's defining elements—flat fields of undifferentiated color, a restricted palette, decorative patterning, and a taut line—seem to evolve from contemporaneous Jain painting. In these Rajput paintings, however, the drawing is more descriptive and the space more perceptible, although shallow and friezelike. The Hindu court literature illustrated includes the tenth chapter of the *Bhagavata Purana* (Ancient stories of Lord Vishnu) dealing with the life of Krishna, a text that would continue to be extremely popular with artists and patrons throughout the history of Indian painting (fig. 4); the *Gita Govinda* (Song of the herdsman); and systemizations of human experience, such as *ragamalas* (garlands of musical modes), *Chaurapanchasika, Rasamanjari* (Essence of the experience of delight), and *Rasikapriya* (Garden of delights). With their audacious linear dynamism and compositional intricacy, these illustrations pique the viewer's senses irresistibly.

The paintings mirror the Hindu world view of a transcendent cosmic order in which myths and symbols are the appropriate subjects of art. They are populated by gods, heroes, and heroines whose depictions are based not on living models but on formulas melding ideals drawn from nature—for example, heads shaped like eggs, chests like a lion's, breasts like ripe mangoes. Colors are limited and chosen for their evocative potential rather than for verisimilitude. As in Indian sculpture, predominantly a tradition of high relief, the space is shallow: figures exist within a matrix and can move neither toward nor away from the viewer. Dynamic drawing and abundant pattern create a sense of surface energy. With these means the Hindu painter conjures an entire, emotionally resonant universe. Although Hindu painting absorbed numerous influences from without over the succeeding centuries, these traditional Rajput pictorial devices reasserted themselves over and over again.

Figure 4. Detail of *Krishna Battles the Armies of the Demon Naraka,* page from a dispersed *Bhagavata Purana* (Ancient stories of Lord Vishnu), ca. 1520–30. Probably Delhi-Agra area. Chaurapanchasika style. See cat. no. 4.

The sixteenth century witnessed one of the most momentous cultural events in the subcontinent's history, the conquest of North India by the Mughals, an Islamic dynasty of Turko-Mongol ancestry descended directly from both Tamerlane and Genghis Khan. For the following century and a half the Mughal court was India's most innovative and powerful center; its impact on the cultural life of the courts of northern India was enormous during its heyday and thereafter as well. The court's fundamentally worldly concept of man and history supported a realistic art that was quite the opposite of the Hindus' art. The intermingling of Mughal and Rajput styles meant the penetration of a new world view into Indian life that allowed everyday events to be invested with a significance heretofore reserved for the divine.

The transformation began in 1526 when Babur, the first of the Mughal line, descended into India from his small Afghani kingdom and conquered the Lodi Sultan of Delhi, establishing sovereignty over a large part of northern India. Babur died in 1530 and was succeeded by his twenty-two-year-old son Humayun (r. 1530–40, 1555–56), who ruled for only eleven years before he was expelled from India by Sher Shah (r. 1540–45), an Afghan adventurer. Humayun took refuge in Tabriz in Persia, at the court of his Safavid cousin Shah Tahmasp. Muslim courts placed great emphasis on the production and appreciation of manuscripts, and Humayun became familiar with works of the Tabriz court's highly evolved school of manuscript painting, which featured intricate patterning, jewel-like color, high finish, and a flattened bird's-eye perspective (fig. 5). But in time the shah turned toward greater Islamic orthodoxy (which forbids the making of images), and his interest in his manuscript atelier waned. When Humayun finally left Tabriz to return to Kabul, he hired away two of the shah's finest artists, Mir Sayyid Ali and Abd-as-Samad. In 1555 Humayun recaptured Delhi, but the next year he died, leaving his newly acquired empire to his twelve-year-old son Akbar.

Akbar (r. 1556–1605) had been trained in art and connoisseurship at the Tabriz court of Shah Tahmasp and believed that painting had a prominent role to play in his own court. Within ten years of his accession, a royal manuscript atelier of thirty painters and seventy assistants had been assembled at his new capital of Fatehpur Sikri, west of Agra. This large contingent of artists was of necessity drawn from diverse traditions of Persia, Central Asia, and India. The atelier's first product was a large-format, multivolume manuscript of the *Hamza-nama* (Story of Prince Hamza) (cat. nos. 7, 8). These paintings of the *Hamza-nama* mark a major shift, conceptually and aesthetically, from productions of the Persian court. Each illumination focuses on a single dramatic episode, which retains its primacy even if it is set among a host of subsidiary vignettes. The size not only of the sheet but also of the elements within has increased so dramatically that the painting is no longer the exclusive province of a single viewer, to be held in his hands and lovingly perused; it is bold enough to be appreciated from a distance by several people. (It is conjectured that this large format derives from a tradition of pictorial nomadic tent hangings.) Space is deeper and more tangible now, and nature has begun to be observed and copied. Gestures are dynamic, psychological motivation becomes apparent. A degree of homogeneity was maintained by giving master artists responsibility for the overall design of pages while assigning several artists to different aspects of its execution.

Akbar's spiritual and intellectual interests seem to have undergone a dramatic change in the 1580s after he moved his capital to Lahore, in present-day Pakistan. His manuscript atelier also was transformed, with many paintings now being assigned to individual artists rather than teams. The paintings became more intimate in scale, subdued in color, refined and sumptuous in finish. In this mature Mughal style, space and volume began to be defined by means of light and shade, a technique learned from Western paintings and prints brought to the cosmopolitan Mughal court and formerly unknown in both the Persian and the indigenous Indian styles. Other Western innovations that were adopted are aerial perspective and the use of atmospheric effects to indicate spatial recession (cat. nos. 12, 13).

Contemporaneously, a more provincial version of the imperial court style began to flourish. It featured elements derived from the Mughal style, but in painting and finish it was never of the quality or complexity of imperial painting. Manuscripts in this provincial Mughal style were produced for both Hindu and Muslim patrons. The largest number of them seem to have been made in the last two decades of the sixteenth century and the early years of the seventeenth century, and some of these are now being ascribed to patronage from specific Rajput states such as Amber and Bikaner.[2] Whether they were the work of minor artists who had left the imperial atelier after the completion of the huge *Hamza-nama* project, were painted by Indian artists at the Mughal court, or came about solely because of the diffusion of artistic ideals from the court is not clear.

Painting at the Hindu courts in the early seventeenth century displayed a spectrum of styles that derived in varying degrees from the Chaurapanchasika (traditional Rajput) and Mughal traditions. Although painting is known from only one court in the hill states, Mandi (cat. no. 19), the diverse kingdoms of Rajasthan reveal great activity. Painting in the relatively isolated

Figure 5. Detail of *Bahram Gur Pins the Coupling Onagers* from Shah Tahmasp's *Shah-nama* (Book of kings), fol. 568r, by Mir Sayyid Ali, ca. 1533–35. Tabriz, Persia. Ink, opaque watercolor, and gold on paper. The Metropolitan Museum of Art, New York, Gift of Arthur A. Houghton Jr., 1970 (1970.301.62)

kingdom of Malwa (cat. no. 16) and in Gujarat seems to have grown directly out of the Rajput tradition, which is reflected in the use of space, color, and line. Painting at Mewar shared similar affinities but sometimes incorporated Mughal influence in the form of specific motifs and a somewhat deepened pictorial space (cat. no. 14). In other states, such as Amber, Bikaner (in the first half of the seventeenth century), and Raghugarh, elements of the provincial

Mughal drawing style were melded with the coloristic vibrancy and unmodeled planes of color typical of the Rajput style (cat. no. 15). In still others, such as Bundi (beginning in the last years of the sixteenth century) and Bikaner (in the second quarter of the seventeenth century), contemporaneous Mughal styles seem to have been the dominant influence, leading modes of drawing and coloration to be adopted that were more sophisticated and naturalistic than those of the popular Mughal tradition (cat. nos. 17, 18).

Once produced for a court, manuscripts of this early period often became models for succeeding generations of artists at that court. In some cases we know this was because several generations of artists from a single family used the same preliminary drawings. In other instances artists undoubtedly had access to earlier sets of drawings and simply repeated their compositions, which contained all the requisite elements to portray a particular story or theme. As is to be expected in a conservative society, iconographic correctness was usually more important to the Indian artist than artistic innovation. However, the relative proportions of the pictures' components and the styles in which they were rendered show variations over time.

Akbar's long reign ended when he died in 1605. He was succeeded as Mughal emperor by Salim, his son by an Amber (Rajasthani) princess, who took the name Jahangir (World Seizer). Jahangir (r. 1605–27) divided his time between Lahore and Delhi. He had grown up during the heyday of Akbar's atelier and was a consummate connoisseur of painting; in a work set before him, he claimed, he could identify the hand of any of the court artists, no matter how small the contribution. When Jahangir had been appointed to posts in the provinces he had maintained his own artists, some of the best of whom worked in a Persian-inspired style. His taste was not for the ambitious manuscript projects dealing with historic or mythical events that his father had favored, but rather for highly finished single works that recorded his own experiences. Greater naturalism, a more subdued, less contrived palette, more lyrical compositions, and an increased depth of characterization were the result.[3] The subject matter of paintings made during Jahangir's reign is idiosyncratic and seems quite clearly to reflect his own interests. His finest painters became specialists in particular genres such as portraiture or natural history studies (cat. nos. 20, 21). He also collected miniatures and had them set into albums with elaborately decorated margins. Jahangir probably reduced the size of Akbar's painting atelier on his accession, retaining only the finest of the artists most attuned to his own aesthetic. Some of the best of these—Manohar, Abu'l Hasan, and Govardhan—were the sons of artists from the Akbari atelier and had begun working in the atelier during Akbar's

Figure 6. Detail of *Shah Jahan on a Terrace Holding a Pendant Set with His Portrait,* 1627/28. Mughal. See cat. no. 24.

lifetime.[4] The unneeded artists presumably sought patronage among the lesser nobility of the imperial and Hindu courts.

Jahangir's son Shah Jahan (r. 1627–58) ascended the Mughal throne in 1627. Although he undoubtedly enjoyed painting, he seems to have been less intent on sponsoring it than his father and grandfather: his chief penchants were building and the accumulation of jewels (fig. 6). While (like his grandfather Akbar) he commissioned an illustrated history of his reign, the *Padshah-nama,* in general a decorative approach to painting gained ascendancy, the intellectual probing of the Jahangiri period was lost, and manuscript production lagged. Shah Jahan's love of luxury and decoration was expressed in a group of remarkable albums of both old and new pictures that were assembled at his behest. They were set in pages and the borders lavished with superb drawn or painted images, some carried out by the atelier's finest artists. Despite the emperor's lack of sustained interest, court painting continued throughout his reign, and some *darbar* (royal audience) scenes of great finish and quality were produced, as well as a great number of portraits, many of which glorified the emperor (cat. nos. 22–26). The royal atelier's size may have been reduced once again, for we know that some of the court artists accepted commissions from lesser members of the court to execute both miniatures and wall paintings.[5]

In 1657 Shah Jahan contracted a serious illness. His four sons immediately began to vie for control of the Mughal throne. Although Shah Jahan recovered, in 1658 his son Aurangzeb, who controlled the imperial armies in the Deccan and had routed his brothers, proclaimed himself emperor (r. 1658–1707). He imprisoned his father in the royal apartments of the Agra Red Fort. Shah Jahan's favorite son, Dara Shikoh, fled, but he was captured and executed in 1659.

One of Aurangzeb's justifications for assuming power had been his distaste for Dara Shikoh's heterodox religious beliefs and his own desire to reinforce Muslim orthodoxy in India. His fundamentalism was soon implemented in a series of ordinances intended to bring the predominantly Hindu population of India to heel. These included a prohibition against the building of new non-Muslim religious structures, the destruction of some recently built ones, and the reimposition of the *jizya*, a tax levied on non-Muslims for their military protection by the faithful that had been abolished by Akbar one hundred years before.[6] These ordinances applied mainly to lands directly under Mughal control, thus not (or not directly) the Rajasthani kingdoms. But they did affect areas that were extremely sacred to Hindus and important for pilgrimage, including Mathura and Banaras. Aurangzeb's puritanism also placed the arts in a precarious position: music was banned at the court and there was scant patronage of painting, since the depiction of living things is forbidden by orthodox Muslims. After a preliminary show of interest in his painting atelier (cat. no. 27), Aurangzeb soon ignored it, and many artists, deprived of commissions, left to find new patronage. Natural attrition must also have played a part: many of the finest artists associated with the atelier had been trained in Akbar's time and by now were old men or deceased. Aurangzeb's attention was focused on trying to extend his power. He conducted a foray into Marwar in 1680 and in 1681 began a series of campaigns to subdue the kingdoms of the Deccan that lasted until his death in 1707.

The small Islamic kingdoms located on the great plateau of the Deccan in Central India had flourished since the fourteenth century and had developed independent cultural traditions. Although some of the smaller ones had become tributary states during the reigns of Akbar and Jahangir, the most important kingdoms, Golconda and Bijapur, remained independent until late in the Aurangzeb period. Their rich cultural traditions had roots in Persia and Turkey, and they had never abandoned the love of pattern and rich color of those court styles. Lavender and many hues of gold, used both as a background and for embellishment, are particularly favored in the opulent Deccani color schemes. A picture's individual elements and the patterns that adorn them are decorative, highly stylized, and sometimes unnaturally enlarged. The Mughals' worldly search for artistic realism was not of primary interest in the Deccan. Deccani artists sought instead to express a more inward journey, with mystic and fantastic overtones (cat. nos. 35, 36).

## THE RAJASTHANI RENAISSANCE

The dispersal of artists from Aurangzeb's court that began about 1660 coincided with a great artistic flowering in the Hindu courts of Rajasthan and the Punjab Hills. This was not simply a matter of late Mughal styles being brought to certain of the Rajasthani courts, such as those at Bikaner, Bundi, and Kota. Rather, artists familiar with the Mughal idiom adapted their aesthetic vocabularies and repertoire of subject matter, as well as their artistic skills, to the needs of their new Hindu patrons. In the period after the accession of Aurangzeb, the Rajasthani ateliers mimicked to an unprecedented degree the compositions, coloration, drawing, and even imperial imagery found in Mughal works, but traditional themes continued to be illustrated as well.

Although in the first half of the seventeenth century royal portraits, hunts, and garden parties had occasionally been depicted by painters in Bundi and Kota, that earlier Rajasthani tradition was mainly concerned with the illumination of Hindu religious texts and treatises. From the 1660s on, however, maharajas began to appear in equestrian and group portraits and amid the hunts, garden parties, and court activities that had previously been the province of Mughal imperial images. Pictorial space became deeper and more naturalistic, and artists began to imitate the subtle colors, forms, and textures of transient things (fig. 7). Paintings increased dramatically in size and continued to be produced on a large scale throughout the following century. For Hindu aristocrats to patronize this new style of painting signaled a major shift in their sensibilities and their assimilation, at least

Figure 7. Detail of *Ladies on a Terrace,* by Ruknuddin, 1665. Bikaner, Rajasthan. See cat. no. 32.

partially, of a new world view in which temporal matters were as valid a subject as mythical ones.

We do not know what prompted this cultural shift at this time. The Hindu courts had already been under Mughal hegemony for over a century and during that time had shown little interest in the content of Mughal painting. We can only speculate whether the change was sparked by the new availability of first-class artists and the repertoire of images they brought with them or whether it was, in some instances, a reaction to the cultural intolerance of Aurangzeb's policies. Whatever the reason, by the beginning of the eighteenth century, dress, etiquette, and gardens in the Mughal style had become fashionable at many of the Rajasthani courts.

The Bikaner painting atelier had been heavily influenced by the art of Shah Jahan's court during the period of Karan Singh (r. 1632–69), and the atelier's finest works show the high finish and naturalism of the imperial court style (cat. no. 18). Initially, traditional Hindu texts were illustrated, but Mughal subjects began to be adopted late in Karan Singh's reign (which was early in Aurangzeb's); this trend continued during a period of close contact between Aurangzeb and Karan Singh's youngest son, Anup Singh (r. 1674–98). As a general in the imperial army Anup Singh had spent many years away from Bikaner, particularly in Hyderabad in the Deccan, where he set up a court. Prolonged exposure to the Mughal culture prevalent at neighboring Golconda may have predisposed him to Mughal styles. Anup Singh's finest artist, Ruknuddin, had already been employed in the Bikaner atelier in the 1660s, and many of the other important artists who worked for the Bikaner court were relatives of his. Ruknuddin's art shows a thorough knowledge of Mughal pictorial prototypes and technique; his best paintings, although they lack the psychological depth of the outstanding early Mughal works, still rival the finest products of the imperial court, technically and as aesthetic accomplishments (cat. nos. 32, 33). The interest they display in space, nuanced color, and the tactile quality of objects is comparable to that evident in Mughal painting and represents a more complete integration of the imperial aesthetic than the earlier, similarly influenced Bikaner style.

The extended presence of Rajasthani nobles in the Deccan, first as warriors and then as governors, led to cultural cross-fertilization between the two areas. The Bikaner maharajas continued to hold military posts for the Mughals in the Deccan during the first decades of the next century, and throughout this period artists accompanied them and were inspired by local painting styles. Deccani artists also immigrated to kingdoms in Rajasthan, including Kota and Bikaner. Deccani influence on Bikaner paintings can be observed in the orchidlike palette and the increased prominence of flamboyant decorative motifs. The qualities of Deccani and Bikaner painting are so thoroughly intermixed that it is sometimes difficult to ascribe a painting definitely to either school (cat. no. 34).

During the same late-seventeenth-century period, an extraordinary renaissance occurred in the Rajasthani courts of Bundi and Kota. For both these courts, close political ties to the Mughal court dated from the early seventeenth century. The Kota maharajas were faithful employees of Aurangzeb and served him in the Deccan throughout the later part of the century.[7] Kota had a tradition of royal portraiture that went back to the first quarter of the seventeenth century, and fragments of early hunting scenes are also known.[8] The Bundi raja, Madhu Singh, was on the losing side during Aurangzeb's seizure of power and initially suffered the new emperor's ire, but ultimately he was pardoned. Just as at Bikaner, the ateliers of these Rajput states flourished and took new inspiration from Mughal art in the late seventeenth century, as is evident in the subjects chosen for depiction as well as the borrowing of motifs and compositions (cat. nos. 28–30).

### THE PUNJAB HILLS

At precisely the same period, a revolution in painting also took place in the Punjab Hills. But in contrast to the assimilationist tendency of the Rajasthani ateliers, the Punjab Hills workshops turned their backs on Mughal influence, a rejection in which political sympathies probably played a part. The great tradition of painting in the hills began rather abruptly in the 1660s in the small state of Basohli under the patronage of Raja Sangram Pal (r. 1635–73). Sangram Pal had ascended the Basohli throne at the age of eight and at twelve had been summoned to Shah Jahan's Mughal court, where he became a close friend of Dara Shikoh, the emperor's favorite son, himself a painting aficionado. But it is hard to believe that Sangram Pal would have stayed on good terms with the Mughals after Aurangzeb seized the throne and put his brother Dara Shikoh to death in 1659. We do know that in 1678, shortly after Sangram Pal died, his successor and a confederation of other hill state rajas evicted Aurangzeb's envoy Mirza Ubed Beg, who had made military incursions into their territory.[9]

The Basohli idiom seems quite clearly to reject Mughal conventions in favor of a style solidly within the mainstream of indigenous Rajput tradition, one that appeals directly to the senses by means of color and pattern. The same holds true for subject matter. Pahari (that is, Punjab Hills) paintings mostly illustrate religious texts rather than embracing Mughal subject matter as most of the Rajasthani ateliers had. Portraiture was practiced, but the standard type showed a seated maharaja in profile attended by one or more courtiers, not the hunts, festivals, and *darbar* scenes contemporaneously in vogue in Rajasthan.

The earliest Basohli manuscript is a splendid and totally original set of paintings depicting tantric forms of Devi, the great Hindu goddess who is female energy incarnate (cat. no. 38). Presumably the works were created to serve as meditative images for the maharaja. The paintings, like the martial deity they portray, are extraordinarily powerful. Vibrant colors, exuberant patterns, and rich surface embellishments are combined with a sophisticated drawing style to produce an effect at once forceful and refined. The series is closely followed by a similarly resplendent series, probably by the same artist, illustrating the *Rasamanjari,* a poetic compendium of lovers (cat. no. 39). Where Sangram Pal found a painter so skillful as a draftsman and colorist is unknown. The sophistication of the painting seems to point to Mughal training, but the totally original style cannot easily be reconciled with that background. On the other hand, there is no known local tradition from which such an artist could have arisen.

During the last third of the century, variants of the Basohli style spread to the nearby hill states of Bahu, Bilaspur, Chamba, Mankot, and Guler and remained popular at least through the first quarter of the eighteenth century (cat. nos. 40–43, 46–49).

## MEWAR

Mewar, the most powerful of the Rajput states, had always been distant from the Mughal orbit both politically and culturally. It had proved especially difficult to conquer, and despite considerable warfare it was not until 1615, ten years after Akbar's death and long after all the other important Rajput states had been brought to terms, that an alliance was finally concluded. The agreement upheld the Rajput honor of the maharana of Mewar by exempting him from making necessarily demeaning personal appearances before the emperor.[10]

As at other Rajasthani courts, by the beginning of the eighteenth century painting at Mewar had begun to appropriate Mughal iconography that celebrated the ruler as universal king. The *rana,* or prince, with his golden nimbus (the Mewar house was descended from the sun), occupied center stage in large-scale paintings of hunts, festivals, and *darbar* scenes. Probably because of the size of these works, several artists, each specializing in a particular aspect of the picture, worked together on a single painting. The fact that many of these sheets are signed on the back is further evidence of Mughal influence, since it is Mughal paintings that most often carry an artist's signature.

Stylistically, however, a more traditional Rajput sensibility dominated Mewari painting. Deep pictorial space, nuanced color, and naturalistic drawing never really took hold but rather were absorbed, in fragmented form, into the artist's conservative vision. The high vantage point of bird's-eye perspective, one of the few artistic devices appropriated from the Mughals by Mewari artists, created a steep ground plane on which discrete pictorial elements were decoratively disposed. Usually flat and stylized, these elements are sprinkled over the surface of the picture so that, even when a deep space is indicated by overlapping forms or architectural perspective, they reinforce the flatness of the picture plane. Color is generally saturated and unmodulated (cat. nos. 50–52).

## THE LATER SPREAD OF MUGHAL CULTURE

The arts of the Mughal court underwent a brief, influential, and splendid revival during the reigns of Farrukh Shah (r. 1713–19) and Aurangzeb's grandson, Muhammad Shah (r. 1719–48). Despite the Mughals' dwindling power, Delhi remained a cultural center. Paintings of the period display a cool elegance in which the atmospheric effects, naturalism, and psychological depth of earlier Mughal painting have been replaced by idealized formulations of beauty seen in unnatural light (cat. nos. 53, 54). Court and love scenes predominate. But patronage largely came to an end when Delhi was sacked in 1739 by the Persian Nader Shah, who carried off not only the royal treasury and Shah Jahan's jewel-encrusted Peacock Throne but a large part of the royal library as well. This tragedy forced many artists of the royal atelier to find patronage at Hindu courts. Thus, early-eighteenth-century Mughal styles came to influence powerfully the art of a number of Rajasthani and

Figure 8. Detail of *Rama, Sita, and Lakshmana at the Hermitage of Bharadvaja,* page from a dispersed *Ramayana* (Story of King Rama), ca. 1780. Kangra, Punjab Hills. See cat. no. 62.

20

Pahari courts, particularly those of Kishangarh in Rajasthan and Jasrota and Guler in the Punjab Hills.

In the Rajasthani state of Kishangarh, Mughal influence had especially notable results. Although some earlier painting survives, the Kishangarh school did not reach maturity until the second quarter of the eighteenth century (cat. nos. 55–57). The most important artists in its atelier at that time were Bhavani Das and Nihal Chand. Bhavani Das, a Hindu, came from Delhi in 1719, the year of Muhammad Shah's accession, and became the highest-paid official of the Kishangarh court. It is curious that an artist of such quality did not remain in Delhi. Whether he had worked at the imperial atelier for Farrukh Shah is not known. Nihal Chand was a Muslim who emigrated from Delhi sometime between 1719 and 1726. The early works of both artists demonstrate familiarity with the style, subject matter, and finish of contemporaneous Mughal painting. Drawing on that tradition, they developed moody, evocative portraits set on marble terraces, with panoramic backdrops of water and landscape and large expanses of white. As at the imperial atelier, a cool palette enlivened by patches of hot reds and pinks was favored, and the painting is precise and carefully built up. The style was somewhat transformed in the late 1740s with the accession of Raja Savant Singh (r. 1748–64), whose passion for his court singer, Bani Thani, inspired a new approach to the art. His artists used the stylized physiognomies of the lovers when portraying Krishna and his beloved Radha, who appear in a plethora of paintings that celebrate their love as a metaphor for union with the divine (cat. no. 70). The restrained color and compositions of the Kishangarh atelier provided a perfect foil for depictions of sensuality, and the results are among the best-known images in later Rajasthani painting.

In the Punjab Hills, the Rajput-inspired Basohli style began to be supplanted by Mughal naturalism in the second quarter of the eighteenth century, and close affinities to painting of the contemporaneous court of Muhammad Shah can be observed. The chief proponents of this new idiom were two brothers, Manaku and Nainsukh, who were the greatest Pahari artists of the eighteenth century. Manaku started his career at Guler, working in a transitional style: his drawing (most clearly visible in the preparatory drawings) and color were beginning to move away from the stylized, chromatically saturated Basohli tradition (cat. nos. 46, 47). His late work, cool and more naturalistic, shows that the evolution continued throughout his career (cat. no. 60). The younger Nainsukh became established in the 1740s at Jasrota, where, for his patron, Raja Balwant Singh, he painted and drew extraordinarily refined and psychologically poignant pictures that demonstrate a close observation of nature. Many are studies of the maharaja from life, some are fantastic allegorical pictures of him, and others treat individual Hindu subjects (cat. nos. 58, 59). Coloristically his miniatures show some similarities with works done at the Mughal court of Muhammad Shah, particularly the prominence of white and the sparing use of hot colors. The facial types Nainsukh employed in representing deities also resemble ones in the imperial style (compare cat. nos. 53, 54).

The plunder of Delhi by Nader Shah in 1739 left the Mughal court impoverished and consigned it to political and cultural decline. The Rajasthani courts, which had responded to successive waves of Mughal influence over the last century and a half, now evolved on their own. Mughal subject matter was not entirely abandoned, but, with varying degrees of completeness, artists subtly reintroduced a more Rajput pictorial sensibility. In many cases the color became bolder and less literal. The picture plane grew shallower, and linear, decorative qualities became more pronounced. The expression of these tendencies varied not only from court to court but also within an atelier, from artist to artist. A wide range of quite distinctive styles was the result (see cat. nos. 69–76).

The developments in the Punjab Hills were more conservative. At the courts of Basohli, Chamba, Guler, Jammu, and Kangra a great flowering of painting took place that was very largely a continuation of the work of Manaku and Nainsukh by their children. The brothers had molded their children's artistic personalities, schooling them in an idealized and romantic naturalism whose deep space, cool palette, observed nature, and idealized faces hark back to Mughal models. Curiously, the most salient characteristic of the style— the pervasive use of a naturalistic landscape to mirror and serve as background for both mythic and everyday events (fig. 8)—had received only cursory treatment from the elder generation. Unlike most of Nainsukh's paintings but like those of his elder brother, these late pictures are predominantly illustrations of manuscripts with religious or poetic themes. They reach their pinnacle with a group of lyrical manuscripts produced for the Kangra court of Sansar Chand (r. 1775–1823) (cat. nos. 62–65).

In the late eighteenth and early nineteenth centuries, Mughal painting traditions enjoyed a kind of resurgence under the patronage of the Muslim potentates who established independent kingdoms in North India and the Deccan. Some of the best paintings depict grandees seated on terraces with vast panoramas of buildings and gardens stretching into the distance behind them. Although such images derive from earlier models, this time the landscape, rather than the sitter, commands the viewer's eye (cat. no. 67).

At the same time, the British officers and grandees who had incorporated a large part of the former Mughal empire into Britain's also employed artists who had been trained in Mughal court traditions. Their depictions of flora, fauna, and everyday Indian life represent a marvelous confluence of literal documentation and pictorial imagination (cat. no. 68). Inspired design and bold patterning raise the best of these works, made as album illustrations, into the realm of art. Unlike their Jahangiri ancestors, they are silhouetted against the white of the page rather than set within a fully realized space.

THE WANING OF THE ART

A diversity of styles continued into the nineteenth century in India, but, except for photographic images, which became popular midcentury, no innovative vision arose to influence traditional Rajput artistic sensibilities. The Mughal court, which had been such a dynamic catalyst, was replaced by an absentee British monarch and an omnipresent bureaucracy uninterested in courtly art. Thus the nineteenth century is a period of decline in Indian art, although enlivened by the work of a few distinguished artists. Company painting continued to be produced but was rarely as finely executed or as beautifully composed as it had been in the late eighteenth century. Some of the Pahari ateliers flourished, but sentimentality and polish replaced the inspiration of the previous century. In Rajasthan the important early centers of Rajasthani painting, such as Bikaner, Kota, and Bundi, were still producing some work of quality. In many of these centers Mughal influences had gradually been sloughed off, and artists reverted to more traditionally Rajput color, space, and form. Also during this period several important new ateliers were formed in Rajasthan at some of the smaller principalities, such as Devgarh and Jhilai (cat. nos. 77, 78). These two owed inspiration to, respectively, Mewar and Jaipur, with which they were tied politically, but the brilliance of their productions was due to individual genius rather than to the great tradition. The glorious innovations and experiments of three centuries of Indian painting slowly came to an end as the Indian ruling classes, imitating European forms of conspicuous consumption, abandoned their historic role as patrons.

1. Desai 1990.
2. Beach 1992, p. 184; Glynn 1996, p. 67.
3. Welch 1978, p. 26.
4. Beach 1978, p. 25.
5. Brown 1924, p. 93.
6. Gascoigne 1971, pp. 224, 227–28.
7. Tod 1920, vol. 3, pp. 1489–94 (Bundi), 1523–25 (Kota).
8. Welch 1983, pp. 82–83.
9. *Punjab States Gazetteers* 1910, p. 94; Desai 1985, p. 18.
10. Banerjee 1983, pp. 83–88.

# CATALOGUE

# 1

## THE FOURTEEN AUSPICIOUS DREAMS OF THE JINA'S MOTHER

### Uttar Pradesh: Jaunpur, ca. 1465

Page from a dispersed Jain *Kalpa Sutra* (Book of rituals)
Ink, opaque watercolor, and gold on paper
4⅝ × 11½ in. (11.8 × 29.3 cm)
The Metropolitan Museum of Art, New York
Purchase, Cynthia Hazen Polsky Gift, 1992 (1992.359)

This page is not entirely characteristic of Jain painting: the illumination is larger, the range of color wider, and the ornamentation more elaborate than usual. The work's provenance is Jaunpur in Central India, not Gujarat in Western India, the primary Jain center. Nevertheless, the patterned surface made up of flat, unmodeled forms outlined by wiry black lines, the use mainly of primary colors, the stylized facial type in which the far eye projects beyond the profile (a device derived from earlier painting styles), and the elaborate borders with scrolling foliate designs convey the essence of the Jain style.

# 2

## NANDA AND VASUDEVA

**Delhi-Agra area, ca. 1520–30**
Page from a dispersed *Bhagavata Purana* (Ancient stories
of Lord Vishnu)
Ink and opaque watercolor on paper
6¾ × 9⅜ in. (17.5 × 23.8 cm)
The Metropolitan Museum of Art, New York
Purchase, Anonymous Gift, 1982 (1982.209)

This work and catalogue numbers 3 and 4, three paintings in the Chaurapanchasika style, are from the oldest
surviving *Bhagavata Purana* manuscript. They illustrate
the tenth chapter, which details the life of Krishna, one
of Vishnu's most popular avatars. The other Chaura-
panchasika-style manuscripts are short, and this one,
originally composed of as many as three hundred pages,

of which about two hundred survive, is by far the
largest early manuscript extant. Both it and the much
smaller *Bhagavata Purana* found at Isarda (cat. nos. 5, 6)
are thought to have been produced in the Delhi-Agra
area; it is probably not coincidental that Mathura, the
birthplace of Krishna and an important pilgrimage site
for his devotees, lies between those two cities.

With its multitiered composition, this painting recalls a bas-relief. In the center of the upper register
Nanda and Vasudeva embrace, highlighted by a brilliant
red background—a device that Indian artists often use
to indicate the picture's energy center. Below, two carts
resting by the bank of a stream, starkly set against black,
seem likewise to intertwine, while the swaying flowers
echo the joyous spirit of the human encounter. The
strong patterning of the page is a quintessential aspect
of the Rajput style.

# BRAHMA PROSTRATES HIMSELF BEFORE KRISHNA

**Delhi-Agra area, ca. 1520–30**
Page from a dispersed *Bhagavata Purana* (Ancient stories of Lord Vishnu)
Ink and opaque watercolor on paper
9¼ × 7 in. (23.6 × 17.9 cm)
Collection of Anita Spertus

Nature often embodies the essence of the narrative in Indian painting. In *Brahma Prostrates Himself before Krishna* the tree trunks bend, mimicking the postures of the protagonists, while the extravagant foliage, filled with blossoms, simultaneously mirrors the agitation of the moment and reassures the viewer of nature's benevolent fecundity. The taut forms are outlined by wiry lines that heighten the bristling energy of the image. A backdrop of red like that in the Nanda and Vasudeva illumination (cat. no. 2), but this time stepped, highlights the encounter.

4

## KRISHNA BATTLES THE ARMIES OF THE DEMON NARAKA

**Probably Delhi–Agra area, ca. 1520–30**
Page from a dispersed *Bhagavata Purana* (Ancient stories
of Lord Vishnu)
Ink and opaque watercolor on paper
7 × 9⅙ in. (17.8 × 23.2 cm)
The Metropolitan Museum of Art, New York
Purchase, Lita Annenberg Hazen Charitable Trust Gift,
1985 (1985.34)

In this battle scene, as in the previous painting, a single
event fills the page. To the right the demon king and
his wife sit securely in their two-story palace; to the left
Krishna and his consort arrive, borne by Garuda, the
god's bird vehicle. At the center the great demon army
is arrayed on elephants. Despite the beasts' individual
massiveness, the shallow space of the picture transforms
them into overlapping planes that seem stacked up
rather than solid forms that seem to recede. The rhythmic frieze of hooves, with its energetic draftsmanship,
typifies the dynamism of the style. Because of the limited range of colors, ultimately no single element dis-
tinguishes itself from the whole; the entire picture can
be perceived as pattern.

# 5

## THE GOPIS BESEECH KRISHNA TO RETURN THEIR CLOTHING

**Probably Delhi-Agra area, ca. 1560–65**
Page from the dispersed "Isarda" *Bhagavata Purana*
(Ancient stories of Lord Vishnu)
Ink and opaque watercolor on paper
7⅝ × 10⅛ in. (19.4 × 25.7 cm)
The Metropolitan Museum of Art, New York
Gift of H. Rubin Foundation Inc., 1972 (1972.260)

Like the earlier *Bhagavata Purana* (cat. nos. 2–4), this manuscript found at Isarda is painted in the Chaurapanchasika style; but it is distinctive in its idiosyncratic palette, line of unvarying width, and complex relationship of image to picture frame. Whereas the earlier work's color scheme revolves around heavy, earthy red, yellow, green, and black, the palette of this *Bhagavata Purana* is more varied, quirkier, and brighter and includes sour pinks, acid greens, and clear yellows and reds. The outline has become sharper and less variable in width. In certain images, a somewhat illusionistic space and naturalistic descriptions reveal a consciousness of Mughal art.

In this painting Krishna, the blue god, has stolen the clothes, or in this case the *cholis* (blouses), of the *gopis* as they frolic in a stream. (*Gopis* are female cowherds, the companions and lovers of Krishna.) The *gopis* in the center have recognized their fate and stand naked before him—a metaphorical reference to the openness before god necessary for salvation. In this picture the ground plane has been tilted back to create a sense of spatial recession, establishing a foreground, middle ground, and background. However, as in the earlier series, the edges do not confine the pictorial elements, which spill over onto the margins on all sides. Thus the stream flows in a wide swath from one side to the other of the entire page, disregarding the boundaries that define the space, and the same is true of the cows at the bottom and the trees at the top of the painting.

## 6

### KRISHNA KILLS THE EVIL KING KAMSA'S WASHERMAN

**Probably Delhi-Agra area, ca. 1560–65**
Page from the dispersed "Isarda" *Bhagavata Purana*
(Ancient stories of Lord Vishnu)
Ink and opaque watercolor on paper
7½ × 9⅞ in. (18.9 × 25.1 cm)
Collection of Anita Spertus

Reference: Hutchins 1980, pp. 86–87, fig. 25

This second example from the "Isarda" set depicts Krishna, his white-skinned brother Balarama, and a companion, after Krishna has beheaded the arrogant cloth dyer who had refused to sell them his goods. Above, the cloth dyer's wife raises her arms in alarm.

The swath of river may allude to the use of running water to rinse excess dye from the cloth. In some ways this depiction is more artistically conservative than the previous example. Although a stream cuts across both images, here it runs perpendicular to the earth rather than across it and is parallel to the picture plane rather than forming the picture's middle ground: the lotuses and the figures within it do not occupy a receding space but rather are pressed close to the viewer in a shallow spatial layer. The three figures standing by the shore and the garments hung out to dry above them appear as a frieze, which the Egyptian-like stances reinforce. Instead of looking outward the participants gaze parallel to the picture plane, a convention that keeps the energy contained within the painting.

## MESBAH THE GROCER BRINGS THE SPY PARRAN TO HIS HOUSE

**Mughal: period of Akbar (r. 1556–1605), ca. 1570**
Page from the dispersed *Hamza-nama* (Story of
Prince Hamza)
Ink, opaque watercolor, and gold on cotton
27⅞ × 21⅝ in. (70.8 × 54.9 cm)
The Metropolitan Museum of Art, New York
Rogers Fund, 1924 (24.48.1)

Reference: Dimand 1948, p. 7, fig. 2

Nothing quite prepares the viewer for the scale and immediacy of illustrations from the *Hamza-nama*, the earliest product of the great emperor Akbar's atelier. The text describes the mythic adventures of Prince Hamza, uncle of the prophet Muhammad, in his quest to disseminate Islam throughout the world. The large-scale, extraordinarily ambitious manuscript had fourteen hundred illustrations with facing pages of text. It was divided into fourteen volumes and took fourteen years to complete. The design and coloring of every page was overseen by a single artist, but several craftsmen worked on each illustration. Although influenced by the style of Persian paintings, these images differ in having a principal narrative element that dominates the scene and a composition that reinforces the picture's dramatic intent.

In *Mesbah the Grocer Brings the Spy Parran to His House,* the tiled floors and walls, carpets, hanging armor, and largely frontal architecture are all contained decoratively in a symmetrical composition parallel to the picture plane. The space is opened up, however, by the clarity and solidity of the figures, which have weight and depth and which overlap one another, by the diagonal of the carpet border, and by the implied sight lines of the participants as they look through and out of the space. There is no question that amidst the decorative complexity, at the center of the action, is a psychological drama. Both main figures are brilliantly characterized, the furtive spy with his contorted posture and animated hands and the massive, still grocer, by far the largest person in the painting, glancing suspiciously toward his guest.

33

## ASSAD IBN KARIBA ATTACKS THE ARMY
## OF IRAJ SUDDENLY BY NIGHT

**Mughal: period of Akbar (r. 1556–1605), ca. 1570**
Page from the dispersed *Hamza-nama* (Story of
Prince Hamza)
Ink, opaque watercolor, and gold on cotton
27 × 21¼ in. (68.6 × 54 cm)
The Metropolitan Museum of Art, New York
Rogers Fund, 1919 (18.44.1)

References: Dimand 1948, p. 7 (not illustrated); Lukens 1965,
pp. 44–45, fig. 59

This illustration displays varied characteristics of style found in the immense *Hamza-nama* manuscript for which it was made. The painting is divided into a foreground, a middle ground, and a background, with the figures and objects in each field smaller than those in the field before. Thus, although the space is not totally coherent, an impression of spatial recession is created.

The action is spread across the three zones, but the changes in scale, with the most important scene at the fore, help clarify the narrative. Stylistic elements of Persian inspiration include the ovoid faces with refined features and the stylized rock forms. Some of the faces are more naturalistic, however; they convey that sense of the event's immediacy so highly valued by Mughal artists.

Detail

# PRINCE RIDING ON AN ELEPHANT

**Mughal: period of Akbar (r. 1556–1605)**
Khemkaran
Ink, opaque watercolor, and gold on paper
6⅞ × 7⅝ in. (17.4 × 19.4 cm)
The Metropolitan Museum of Art, New York
Rogers Fund, 1925 (25.68.4)

Artists of several nationalities filled Akbar's atelier, and disparate stylistic elements were often incorporated into a single painting. This page displays the Indian sensibility of its painter in its division into large areas of color and the choice of a flat yellow background. However, the physiognomy of the prince is clearly dependent on Persian prototypes, and the artist's modeling of forms to create the sense of volumes within space, most observable with the elephant, is purely Mughal. Such details as the trunk curling over itself, the foot raised to reveal an ovoid underside, and the tail swishing in front of the saddle blanket contradict the work's decorative flatness, suggesting a space deeper than that in contemporaneous Rajput painting, where pictorial elements rarely break out of a plane. The artist is interested as well in conveying to the viewer the texture, movement, and weight of the objects he describes rather than presenting idealized images of them.

## 10

### ROYAL RIDING HORSE AND RUNNER

**Mughal: period of Akbar (r. 1556–1605)**
Ink, opaque watercolor, and gold on paper
6½ × 9¼ in. (16.4 × 24.7 cm)
The Metropolitan Museum of Art, New York
Fletcher Fund, 1925 (25.68.3)

The elegant arabesques of the design, the kindred textures of the horse's dappled coat and the fantastic rocky landscape, and the stereotyped physiognomy of the groom, with ovoid head, large chin, dark eyes, small nose, and bowlike mouth, are some of the features indicating that the painter of this miniature was trained in the Persian style. The edges of the forms modulate from light to dark, creating a continuously changing visual interplay between the horse and the background, like that seen in nature. Although the horse and groom exist within a narrow space, the setting is a deep landscape.

11

## KRISHNA AND BALARAMA FIGHT THE ENEMY

**Mughal: probably Lahore, period of Akbar (r. 1556–1605), ca. 1590–95**
Page from a dispersed *Harivamsa* (Genealogy
of Vasudeva Krishna)
Ink, opaque watercolor, and gold on paper
11⅛ × 7½ in. (29.4 × 19.9 cm)
The Metropolitan Museum of Art, New York
Purchase, Edward C. Moore Jr. Gift, 1928 (28.63.3)

Akbar was fascinated by various religions and ultimately formulated his own eclectic faith. A number of
Hindu epics were translated and illustrated in his ate-

lier. It is interesting to compare this page with catalogue number 4, which illustrates a similar scene. Both
images convey the might of the opposing armies by
presenting a mass of warriors, but their treatments of
space differ radically. In the early work space is shallow
and difficult to read. Here, however, the recession of
forms in space is clearly conveyed: it begins with the
foreground melee, articulated by means of contrasting
pattern, color, and tone; continues into the relatively
uncluttered middle ground, where the blue-skinned
Krishna aims his arrow at the enemy; and concludes in
a deep landscape in which the opposing troops muster.
The artist has not yet adopted atmospheric recession or
chiaroscuro, two European painterly methods that
were soon to enter the repertoire of Mughal artists.

## BAHRAM GUR WATCHING DILARAM CHARM THE WILD ANIMALS WITH HER MUSIC

**Mughal: probably Lahore, period of Akbar (r. 1556–1605), ca. 1595**
Attributed to Miskin
Page from the *Hasht Behesht* (Eight paradises) of Amir Khosrow Dihlavi
Ink and opaque watercolor on paper
9⅝ × 6 in. (24.5 × 15.1 cm)
The Metropolitan Museum of Art, New York
Gift of Alexander Smith Cochran, 1913 (13.228.28)

Miskin was one of the greatest artists of Akbar's court. His work is distinguished by the arabesque that animates every element in his complex compositions. This illustration of a Persian text displays the intimate scale and refined execution of manuscripts made for the Lahore court. It is indebted to Persian prototypes in its figure types, stylized horses, and fantastic rock formations, but the deep space, atmospheric recession, and chiaroscuro derive from European models. By this period the Mughal atelier clearly had assimilated these disparate elements into a unified style and was moving toward artistic maturity. Modulated tone replaces flat blocks of color in an effort to reproduce the seen, rather than the conceptualized, world. The image is no longer experienced as pattern and all at once; it slowly unfolds, incorporating the element of time and thus involving the observer, who can traverse the clearly delineated space. Anecdotal descriptions of nature are everywhere to be relished but are secondary to the main event. The finish is both free and extraordinarily refined. A sense of freshness and intimacy pervades the work.

## HAMID BHAKARI PUNISHED BY AKBAR

**Mughal: probably Lahore, period of Akbar
(r. 1556–1605), ca. 1604**
Attributed to Manohar
Page from the dispersed *Akbar-nama* (Chronicle of Akbar)
Ink, opaque watercolor, and gold on paper
8⅞ × 5⅛ in. (22.6 × 13 cm)
The Metropolitan Museum of Art, New York
Theodore M. Davis Collection, Bequest of Theodore M.
Davis, 1915 (30.95.174.7)

Reference: Beach 1981, pp. 103, 120

This brilliantly rendered page by another of Akbar's finest artists commemorates a massive four-day hunt and slaughter that took place in 1567. The superb design conveys the frenzied panic of the doomed animals as they flee the mighty emperor but also achieves a sense of aesthetic equilibrium in which Akbar is the fulcrum. The emperor's resolve is contrasted with the suffering face of the wayward courtier Hamid Bhakari, who is paraded in the foreground with his head shaved in penance. Bhakari was granted a reprieve from decapitation only when, fatefully, Akbar's sword failed to injure him. Thus the scene in its entirety highlights the emperor's sovereignty over life and death. The psychological depth, subtle modeling, and nuanced palette of this painting are typical of the finest works from the last years of Akbar's reign.

Detail

## KHAMBHAVATI RAGINI

**Rajasthan: Mewar, Chawand, 1605**
Nasir ud-Din
Page from the dispersed "Chawand" *Ragamala* series
(Garland of musical modes)
Ink and opaque watercolor on paper
7¼ × 7¼ in. (19.8 × 18.3 cm)
San Diego Museum of Art
Edwin Binney 3rd Collection (1990.0587)

Reference: Binney and Archer 1968, p. 18, no. 2, ill.

Indian music uses the *raga,* a musical phrase, as the basis for improvisations that evoke a spiritual response in the listener. Each *raga* is associated with a specific mood, time of day, and season. Many *ragas* have counterparts in poetry or the visual arts that are set in de-votional or romantic milieus, with religious overtones. The painted systemizations of *ragas,* or *ragamalas,* are hieratically organized into "families" of father (*raga*), wives (*raginis*), sons (*ragaputras*), and daughters (*ragaputris*). This *ragini* shows the Hindu god Brahma, who holds a manuscript, prayer beads, and mace, being worshiped in a court setting by a lady.

The page was part of a set, which, because its colophon survives, we know was painted in 1605 by a Muslim artist at the temporary Mewari capital of Chawand (Chitor fort had been destroyed by Akbar, and Udaipur was yet to be built). It is the earliest known *ragamala* series from Mewar. The style of this picture derives from sixteenth-century Rajput painting, but the line has become less vigorous and the patterning more restrained. Except for the highest finial of the palace, the picture's contents do not break the frame.

## KRISHNA FLUTING

**Rajasthan: probably Amber, ca. 1610**
Page from the dispersed "Boston" *Rasikapriya* (Garden
of delights)
Ink and opaque watercolor on paper
9 × 5⅝ in. (22.9 × 14.3 cm)
The Metropolitan Museum of Art, New York
Rogers Fund, 1918 (18.85.5a)

The monsoon has arrived and Krishna is greeting it
joyfully by singing, dancing, and playing his flute, accompanied by two musicians who play a drum and
hand cymbals. The god wears a skirt and a crown of
peacock feathers. The peacocks, his friends, are drawn
to him and join him in display at this auspicious moment. To the right, two demure, gentle *gopis* attend the
festivities. The text above describes the appearance and
demeanor of Krishna and the *gopis,* presenting them as
an ideal hero (*nayaka*) and ideal heroines (*nayikas*).

The manuscript from which this painting comes has
long been regarded as a provincial Mughal work; only
recently has an Amber provenance been suggested on
the basis of close similarities between the architecture
depicted in this series and in two *ragamala* series, one
from about 1630 and a second dated 1709 and known
to be from Amber.[1] Few paintings had previously been
assigned to the Amber court. An origin in Amber is
not unlikely, since Akbar married an Amber princess
and there were close political ties between the early
Mughals and the Amber rajas.

1. Beach 1992, pp. 184–85; Glynn 1996, pp. 67–68 n. 4.

## RAGINI KAKUBHA

**Rajasthan: Malwa, ca. 1630–35**
Page from a dispersed *Ragamala* series (Garland of
musical modes)
Ink, opaque watercolor, and gold on paper
7⅜ × 6¼ in. (18.7 × 15.9 cm)
Collection of Anita Spertus

Reference: Welch 1973, p. 36, no. 13, ill.

This painting, which achieves a kind of visual poetry,
comes from one of the most beautiful of the early
Malwa manuscripts. Distraught because of separation
from her lover, the maiden Kakubha, her hair un-
plaited, has slipped out at night to the forest. There,
amidst the rain and lightning, she holds flower garlands
and is surrounded by plaintive peacocks. As is the case
in the "Chawand" *Ragamala* (cat. no. 14), the shallow
space and limited color range of the Chaurapanchasika
style are still apparent but the strongly linear drawing
style has been abandoned. The staccato quality of the
early pictures has been replaced by a more lyrical mode
in which a gentle asymmetry reigns within the square
confines of the frame.

## 17

### A ROYAL HORSE WITH HIS GROOM

**Rajasthan: Bundi, ca. 1640**
Ink and opaque watercolor on paper
6¾ × 9½ in. (17.1 × 24.2 cm)
The Kronos Collections

The Bundi painting tradition was one of the earliest to be directly inspired by Mughal prototypes. That influence can be seen in the highly specific descriptive detail that makes this not a generic representation but the portrait of a particular horse, his restless spirit tellingly conveyed. However, the red border, unmodulated yellowish background, and dynamic line evoke traditional Hindu painting, as does the relatively shallow space. Although the colors are softer than those of the earlier Rajput tradition, they are still applied mainly in flat areas. The drawing line is more controlled and more varied than it was earlier. Dynamic line was to become one of the hallmarks of the related Bundi and Kota schools; it is interesting to note its early appearance here. This portrait is constructively compared with the Akbari paintings of a prince riding an elephant and a horse with a runner (cat. nos. 9, 10).

45

## PANCHAMA RAGINI

**Rajasthan: Bikaner, ca. 1640**
Page from a dispersed *Ragamala* series (Garland of
musical modes)
Ink, opaque watercolor, and gold on paper
7¾ × 4⅞ in. (19.7 × 12.3 cm)
The Metropolitan Museum of Art, New York
Purchase, Patricia Phelps de Cisneros Gift, in honor of
Mahrukh Tarapor, 1996 (1996.378)

In this illustration of a musical mode, a maidservant
holding a peacock-feather fly whisk attends a raja and
his consort in a pavilion, while on the terrace outside,
two musicians receive payment from the raja. Judging
from the painting's quality of drawing, color, and execution, Karan Singh of Bikaner (r. 1632–69) must have
enriched his atelier with artists who worked or trained
at the Mughal imperial atelier. The richly gilded, finely
detailed, elaborately patterned textiles are described
with great beauty, as is the light falling on the trees beyond the enclosure. Close observation of nature is evident, as well as an intent to capture psychology and
gesture. The raja's features are so similar to those in two
later drawings of Karan Singh that it may be a portrait.
In contrast to this naturalism, the architectural setting
of red sandstone and marble and the blinds that cover
the portals exist in a limited space in which spatial recession is only weakly implied, and the perspective of
the two foreground steps is poorly understood.

## 19

## A MARRIAGE PROCESSION IN A BAZAAR

**Punjab Hills: Mandi, ca. 1645**
Attributed to the Early Mandi Master
Ink and opaque watercolor on paper
12⅝ × 19¼ in. (32 × 49 cm)
Collection of Howard Hodgkin

References: Glynn 1983, p. 53, fig. 13; Topsfield and Beach
1991, pp. 50–51, no. 25

Little early-seventeenth-century painting from the Punjab Hills survives; but, curiously, the maker of this work, who was employed at the Mandi court, was responsible for some of the most ambitious and successful Rajput paintings of the period. This master's oeuvre includes portraits, illustrations of a *ragamala* set, pages from *Bhagavata Purana* and *Ramayana* manuscripts, and three pictures of a marriage ceremony, of which this is the first page. Many of these works are oversized compared to other paintings of the period, and the three in this set are the largest of all. The painter's indebtedness to Mughal prototypes is clear. He exhibits not only Mughal-type attitudes toward color, space, composition, and the observation of natural events but a kindred interest in psychology as well. The apple-green ground of the picture, probably produced from malachite, and the fine finish of the surface are also likely to have derived from contemporaneous Mughal practice.

## 20

### NILGAI (BLUE BULL)

**Mughal: period of Jahangir (r. 1605–27), ca. 1620**
Mansur
Leaf from an album made for the emperor Shah Jahan
Ink, opaque watercolor, and gold on paper
7⅛ × 9½ in. (18.2 × 24.2 cm)
The Metropolitan Museum of Art, New York
Purchase, Rogers Fund and The Kevorkian Foundation
Gift, 1955 (55.121.10.13)

Reference: Welch et al. 1987, pp. 178–79, no. 47, ill.

Mansur, the "wonder of the age," began his career in Akbar's atelier but perfected his extraordinary natural-history painting during Jahangir's reign. He became the emperor's constant traveling companion in order to record visually the natural phenomena that fascinated his master. As Jahangir wrote in his diary, his great-grandfather Babur had only described what he saw, while he himself also ordered drawings to be made of the things he wrote about, so that "the amazement that arose from hearing of them might be increased."[1] This famous, subtly colored study of a bull antelope does not simply provide a taxonomically clear portrait of a particular animal (note the broken horn). It also conveys to the viewer the texture of the creature's fur, bone, horn, and flesh, as well as its gentle spirit, which radiates from the glassy eye and contented expression. Although the background is barely indicated, the contour of the *nilgai* is so beautifully modulated that the animal's form interacts seamlessly with the space surrounding it.

1. Gascoigne 1971, p. 134.

## PRINCE KHURRAM (SHAH JAHAN) WITH HIS SON DARA SHIKOH

**Mughal: period of Jahangir (r. 1605–27), ca. 1620**
Nanha
Leaf from an album made for the emperor Shah Jahan
Ink, opaque watercolor, and gold on paper
15⅜ × 10⅜ in. (39 × 26.2 cm)
The Metropolitan Museum of Art, New York
Purchase, Rogers Fund and The Kevorkian Foundation
Gift, 1955 (55.121.10.36)

Reference: Welch et al. 1987, pp. 194–95, no. 55, ill.

This superbly painted image framed by a splendid border shows the future emperor with his favorite son, admiring jewels. The father, holding a tray of emeralds and rubies, contemplates a ruby in his right hand, while the child grasps a peacock fan and a turban ornament. They are seated on a raised dais that is placed at an uncharacteristic diagonal to the picture plane. Both father and son are turned toward the viewer, but, as with most Mughal portraits, their heads are seen in strict profile. The sumptuousness of court life is conveyed in the detailed depiction of the jewels, the gilded furniture, the textiles, and, most spectacularly, the large bolster—a tour de force—with its design of figures and plants. The asymmetry of the page and the playing off of a naturalistic scene against a large expanse of mostly undifferentiated background are especially strong design elements. In many ways these features particularly relate to a traditional Rajput sensibility, which undoubtedly informs this work. The composition is further enhanced by the beautiful border, whose flora and fauna are unusually varied and freely disposed.

## AKBAR, WITH LION AND HEIFER

**Mughal: period of Shah Jahan (r. 1627–58), ca. 1630**
Govardhan
Leaf from an album made for the emperor Shah Jahan
Ink, opaque watercolor, and gold on paper
15⅜ × 10⅛ in. (38.9 × 25.6 cm)
The Metropolitan Museum of Art, New York
Purchase, Rogers Fund and The Kevorkian Foundation
Gift, 1955 (55.121.10.22)

Reference: Welch et al. 1987, pp. 96–97, no. 9, ill.

Allegorical portraits based on English prototypes constitute an important genre that emerged at Jahangir's court and continued, in a somewhat more restrained mode, into the reign of Shah Jahan. Mughal realism's keen observation of nature is brought into play in these pictures, and fantastic subjects are made plausible by their precisely rendered detail and an overall spatial harmony. Here Akbar (1542–1605) is shown holding a string of prayer beads while leaning on a sheathed sword. The lion and cow are clearly a transmuted version of the lion and lamb, symbols of a peaceable kingdom. Two putti serenade the emperor from the sky, while a third holds aloft a European-style crown. Govardhan was one of the finest painters to work in the imperial atelier since the period of Akbar; here his knowledge of European painting, also evident in the atmospheric rendition of landscape and the use of chiaroscuro, is combined with a characteristically Mughal interest in psychological portraiture. Perhaps Govardhan drew on studies made of the emperor during his lifetime to distill this insightful portrait.

21

عمل گوردهن

॥श्रीभैरवीदेवी॥

23

## SHRI BHAIRAVI DEVI

**Mughal: period of Shah Jahan (r. 1627–58), ca. 1630**
Attributed to Payag
Ink, opaque watercolor, and gold on paper
7¼ × 10⅜ in. (18.5 × 26.5 cm)
Private collection
Courtesy of the Arthur M. Sackler Museum,
Harvard University Art Museums

Reference: Welch 1995, pp. 293, 325–28, 330–32, 334–35,
357, pl. 19, fig. 13

Although Akbar commissioned a number of manuscripts on Hindu subjects, later Mughal paintings of Hindu subjects are rare. This single page illustrates a horrific form of the Devi and was painted by one of the premier artists of the imperial atelier. Notations on its reverse attest that it was in the royal collection of Mewar. It may have been commissioned as a royal gift to the *rana* of Mewar, who, like most Rajputs, worshiped the Devi (the great goddess, called Bhavani). Perhaps the painting was intended as a gift for Maharana Jagat Singh, who had protected the future Shah Jahan from the wrath of his father, Jahangir, but who died only two months after Shah Jahan became emperor.

The horrific goddess is shown in a cremation ground with her ash-smeared consort, Shiva, who appears as a *sadhu* (beggar). Huge crematory fires burn and skeletal parts litter the glowing ground, but the page is dominated by the bloodred four-armed goddess sitting on the corpse of a victim and holding his head aloft in one hand, a sword in another. Her head is encircled by golden nimbuses; blood spills from her mouth. Despite the grisly trappings, this is an image of cosmic order restored.

## SHAH JAHAN ON A TERRACE HOLDING A PENDANT SET WITH HIS PORTRAIT

**Mughal: period of Shah Jahan (r. 1627–58),**
**dated 1627/28**
Chitarman
Leaf from an album made for the emperor Shah Jahan
Ink, opaque watercolor, and gold on paper
15⅓ × 10⅛ in. (38.9 × 25.6 cm)
The Metropolitan Museum of Art, New York
Purchase, Rogers Fund and The Kevorkian Foundation
Gift, 1955 (55.121.10.24)

Reference: Welch et al. 1987, pp. 198–201, no. 58, ill.

Shah Jahan's love of intimate sumptuous objects is doubly manifest in this extraordinary portrait, probably made as an imperial gift. The work clearly grows out of the fantastic allegorical portraits of Jahangir, especially in the treatment of the sky, where the clouds, inhabited by putti, receive color from, and draw back to frame, the glorious radiance of the monarch's sunlike nimbus. The technique and finish of the painting are superb. Great pains have been taken to render tactile as well as visual qualities: the viewer senses the subtle contrasts between the flowered gauze of the emperor's tunic, his heavy gold sash, and his spinel-studded strings of pearls. Each element seems realized to an almost supra-human degree. The conceit that has the emperor holding a miniature portrait of himself further intensifies the impact of this tour de force of illusionism. The beautifully considered borders perfectly enhance the miniature by extending the glow of blue and gold to the edges of the page.

## 25

## SHAH JAHAN WATCHING AN ELEPHANT FIGHT

**Mughal: period of Shah Jahan (r. 1627–58), ca. 1639**
Bulaqi
Page from the dispersed *Padshah-nama* (History of
the emperor)
Ink, opaque watercolor, and gold on paper
15 × 9¾ in. (38.2 × 24.7 cm)
The Metropolitan Museum of Art, New York
Harris Brisbane Dick, Louis V. Bell, Pfeiffer and
Dodge Funds, 1989 (1989.135)

This fine page from the *Padshah-nama* is typical of the high-quality work that continued to emerge from the imperial atelier. The artist has created a unified space stretching from the foreground, where goaders are milling, to the top of the scene, where the emperor and his two sons are shown in profile at an open tripartite window. Although the white-and-red walls of the fort are unmodulated planes, the placement of figures before them gives a sense of spatial recession. The dynamism of the elephant combat balances the impassive royal family portraits. While the courtiers in the upper tier turn their backs on the melee to face the royals and the lower ones seem more concerned with the combat, curiously, none of them look directly at the object of their attention, somewhat diminishing the work's psychological intensity. Nevertheless, the artist subtly suggests that the emperor, under his gilded roof, is the lord of all beneath him.

## 26

## SHAMSA (ROSETTE) BEARING THE NAME AND TITLES OF THE EMPEROR SHAH JAHAN

**Mughal: period of Shah Jahan (r. 1627–58), ca. 1645**
Leaf from an album made for the emperor Shah Jahan
Ink, opaque watercolor, and gold on paper
15⅜ × 10½ in. (39.1 × 26.7 cm)
The Metropolitan Museum of Art, New York
Purchase, Rogers Fund and The Kevorkian Foundation
Gift, 1955 (55.121.10.39r)

References: Welch 1984, pp. 236–37, no. 155, ill.; Welch et
al. 1987, pp. 80–81, no. 1, ill.

This superb *shamsa*, or little sun, is a lattice of stylized foliate and floral motifs surrounded by phoenixes and other birds flying amid Chinese-style clouds. It forms a spatial setting for the central calligraphy, which reads, "His Majesty, Shihabuddin Muhammad Shah Jahan, the King, Warrior of the Faith, may God perpetuate his kingdom and sovereignty." The page epitomizes Shah Jahan's love of the sumptuous and precious. The intense jewel-like colors and intricately woven arabesques of the central rosette find their closest parallels in contemporaneous carpets, while the gilt drawings beyond it, freed from the usual restraints of a rectangular margin, are particularly fluid and harmonious. The album at the Metropolitan Museum, for which this *shamsa* was made, includes another *shamsa* page in which the calligraphy of the central cartouche was obliterated by a teardrop-shaped stamped seal impression containing the titles of Aurangzeb, Shah Jahan's usurper son.

25

26

## 27

### AURANGZEB WITH HIS THIRD SON, SULTAN AZAM

**Mughal: period of Aurangzeb (r. 1658–1707)**
Attributed to Hunhar
Ink, opaque watercolor, and gold on paper
7½ × 8⅜ in. (19.1 × 21.4 cm)
Private collection
Courtesy of the Arthur M. Sackler Museum,
Harvard University Art Museums

References: Welch 1978, pp. 112–13, pl. 37; Beach 1992,
pp. 150, 155, 163, fig. 117

This painting, perhaps made by the premier artist of Aurangzeb's court, was done early in the emperor's reign and shows that initially, production at the imperial atelier continued as it had during the previous period. The hieratic composition is set beneath a sumptuous symmetrical canopied enclosure, with the space between the emperor and the falcon he holds acting as a fulcrum. All the figures, even the falcon, are shown in profile, like stage flats, except for Aurangzeb's young son, who stands across from the emperor. He stares at his father with his head and body turned outward, breaking the confines of the picture plane and relieving the rigid formality of the composition. In the painting's opulent palette golds and oranges predominate, offset by the cool blue of the sky and an unusual amount of black. A portion of the bottom of the picture has probably been lost.

## 28

## RAO RATON OF BUNDI

**Rajasthan: Bundi, ca. 1660**
Ink, opaque watercolor, and gold on paper
7⅞ × 10 in. (20 × 25.3 cm)
Collection of Dr. Alvin O. Bellak

In 1635 Rao Raton (r. ca. 1606–58) and his two sons gained particular favor with the emperor Jahangir by putting down a rebellion in the Deccan begun by the emperor's son Prince Khurram and supported by many of the other Rajput princes. Rao Raton's prowess in battle was legendary. This posthumous portrait of the ruler shows him controlling a particularly spirited stallion, attended by a retainer and a foot soldier. Despite the Mughal influence evident in the portraiture and in such details as the turned-up hoof, transparent muslin, and apple-green background, the painting's chief inspiration is from traditional Rajput art: the space is frieze-like, the figures are shown in profile and overlap the borders, the color is unmodulated, and a whiplash line—no doubt a late variant, stylistically, of sixteenth-century draftsmanship—fills the page with an energy akin to that of its predecessors.

29

## RAO JAGAT SINGH I IN HIS GARDEN

**Rajasthan: Kota, ca. 1670**
The Kota Master
Ink, opaque watercolor, gold, and silver on paper
10½ × 7⅜ in. (26.7 × 18.7 cm)
The Knellington Collection
Courtesy of the Arthur M. Sackler Museum,
Harvard University Art Museums

References: Dickson and Welch 1981, vol. 1, p. 232–33,
fig. 282; Welch 1983, pp. 79, 81, 82, figs. 5, 6; Welch 1984,
pp. 357–58, no. 241, ill.; Beach 1992, pp. 163, 164, fig. 124

Rao Jagat Singh I, smoking a hookah, is seated on a raised platform set on a round marble slab in the center of his garden. He is attended by two women bearing cooling refreshments and one with a fly whisk. Axially arranged gardens divided by water channels and pools with fountains were introduced into India by the Mughals, who borrowed the idea from Persian examples in which the arrangement was thought to mimic paradise. Thus in this painting both the notion of portraiture and the plan of the garden were inspired by Mughal taste, with which the *rao*, who served Aurangzeb in the Deccan throughout the late seventeenth century, was well acquainted. However, the painting's execution and its depiction of space are allied to the Rajput sensibility. The ground plane is tilted straight up parallel to the picture plane, pressing the garden's lush foliage and water channels forward toward the viewer. Only the figures at the center of the composition exist in a narrow space. As with many great Rajasthani paintings, the mood of the work is haughty and spirited.

30

## TWO ELEPHANTS FIGHTING

**Rajasthan: Kota, ca. 1670**
The Kota Master
Ink and opaque watercolor on paper
13½ × 27⅛ in. (34.2 × 69 cm)
Collection of Howard Hodgkin

References: Beach 1974, pp. 32–33, fig. 75; Welch 1976,
pp. 88–89, no. 44a, ill.; Topsfield 1984, pp. 31, 35, fig. 24;
Cimino 1985, p. 91, no. 90, ill.; Topsfield and Beach 1991,
pp. 48–49, no. 14, ill.

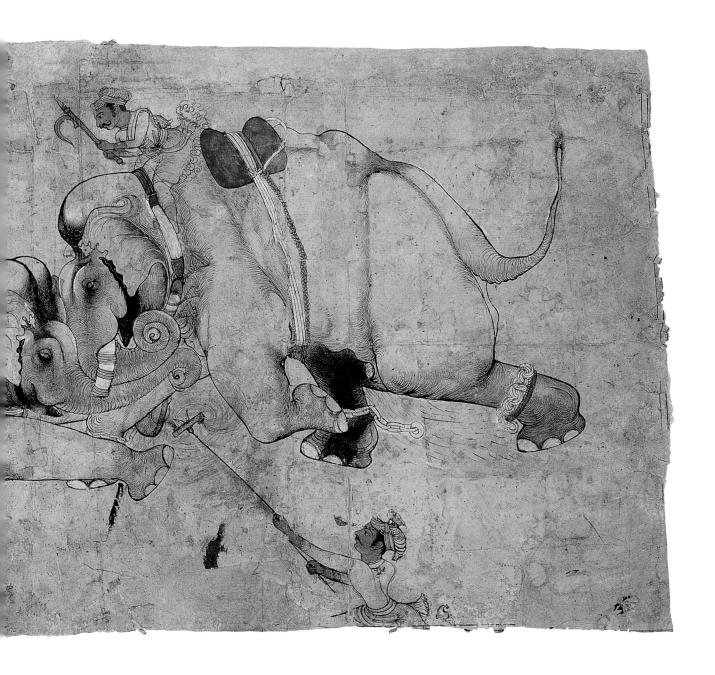

This large-scale drawing of clashing elephants exhibits a dynamism typical of the best traditional Rajput art. It dates from the reign of Rao Jagat Singh I (r. 1657–84). His atelier's master artist produced works whose compositions and iconography derived from Mughal models; they in turn served as the basis for many later Kota paintings. Despite its stock Mughal composition (see cat. no. 25), this work demonstrates its maker's keen observation of nature, another Mughal preoccupation.

Craggy masses of elephant flesh are conjured by parallel pen strokes reminiscent of the parallel lines in European engravings. Volume is also suggested by the varied density and speed of the outline and by areas of deep shade, while the internal movement of flesh and bone is beautifully realized. The viewer senses the velocity of the beast on the right and the crushing impact as it lunges into its opponent. Elephant combats were a favorite sport of Indian princes.

## RAO BHOJ SINGH OF BUNDI SLAYS
## A LION

**Rajasthan: Kota, ca. 1720**
Attributed to the Kota Master
Ink and opaque watercolor on paper
18¾ × 26 in. (47.6 × 66 cm)
Collection of Stuart Cary Welch
Courtesy of the Arthur M. Sackler Museum,
Harvard University Art Museums

References: Welch and Beach 1965, pp. 48, 77, 120,
no. 31, ill.; Beach 1974, pp. 35–37, figs. 86, 87; Dickson
and Welch 1981, vol. 1, pp. 233–34, figs. 283, 284; Welch
1983, pp. 84, 85, figs. 9, 10; Welch 1984, p. 365, no. 245, ill.

In this splendid painting the prowess of Rao Bhoj
Singh, one of the greatest ancestral warrior-rajas of
the Bundi-Kota clan, is pitted against two ferocious,
gigantic lions roaming an untamed wilderness. The
line that defines the forms is almost calligraphic and
has become a decorative force in its own right. This
is most clearly the case with the highly stylized lions, but it is also discernible in the varied textures
of the seething forest. The Kota Master may have
been trained in the Deccani state of Golconda;
both the energetic line and the diagonal composition of this work are features found in Golconda
painting, which in turn derived from Turkoman
prototypes. Animated depictions of beasts in combat constitute some of the greatest of the Kota
Master's creations. These subjects became a signature feature of the Kota school, and for a century
paintings of this type continued to be the school's
most celebrated productions.

## LADIES ON A TERRACE

**Rajasthan: Bikaner, 1665**
Ruknuddin
Ink, opaque watercolor, and gold on paper
9 × 6 in. (22.7 × 15.1 cm)
The Kronos Collections

Like some other Rajasthani courts closely allied with the Mughals, the court of Bikaner had been assimilating Mughal influences throughout the seventeenth century. The art of painting reached a peak there in the late seventeenth and early eighteenth centuries. This miniature's jewel-like color, refined drawing, extraordinary detail, superb finish, and poetic mood mark it as one of the finest paintings by Ruknuddin, Bikaner's premier artist during the late seventeenth century. In this record of a fleeting moment the artist discloses to the viewer the sensory delights of intimate court pleasures. The scene derives from Mughal paintings of harems that were first made during the reign of Shah Jahan but continued to be popular in the Aurangzeb period. At least one other closely related painting is known; the two may have been part of a set.[1]

1. Randhawa and Galbraith 1968, p. 99, pl. 19 (dated 1666).

33

## KEDAR RAGINI

**Rajasthan: Bikaner, ca. 1690–95**
Ruknuddin
Page from a dispersed *Ragamala* series (Garland of
musical modes)
Ink, opaque watercolor, and gold on paper
6 × 4¾ in. (15.2 × 12.1 cm)
The Metropolitan Museum of Art, New York
Gift of Mr. and Mrs. Peter Findlay, 1978 (1978.540.2)

This image of two aspects of Kedar Ragini brings together two disparate interpretations. In one text she is
described as a woman who has taken the form of an
ash-smeared yogi and who, playing a *vina,* sings mourn-
fully of her lover. Another source describes Kedar as a
young male devotee of Shiva who meditates on the
god, wears a snake as an ornament, and sits beneath a
crescent moon. Although the conservative tradition of
*Ragamala* painting usually dictates a somewhat static
composition, Ruknuddin has created a poetic image in
which the female and male aspects of the *ragini* are
joined within a subtly colored moonlit landscape dominated by a tall tree. The forms are flatter than in the
earlier painting by the same master (cat. no. 32), and a
timeless sense pervades the still night.

## DEMONS FIGHTING OVER AN ANIMAL LIMB

**Rajasthan: Bikaner or the Deccan, last quarter of the 17th century**
Ink, opaque watercolor, and gold on paper
11⅝ × 7⅜ in. (29.4 × 18.6 cm)
The Metropolitan Museum of Art, New York
Gift of Doris Rubin, in memory of Harry Rubin,
1989 (1989.236.3)

The precise subject of this painting has not been established, nor is its place of execution secure. The extraordinary demons pictured here stand out within the Hindu corpus because of their eccentric coloration, bizarre patterning, and remarkable heads. Fantastic creatures of this type originated in Central Asian manuscripts, which were copied in Persia and ultimately served as models for Islamic court ateliers elsewhere, including those in the Deccan. The exotic color scheme, particularly the extensive use of lavender and mauve, and the peculiar rock forms seem to point to a Deccani provenance. But other elements in the landscape, such as the foreground stream, the women in the middle ground, and the trees and animals, are more in the Bikaner style. Probably the painting was made by an artist of that Rajasthani kingdom who had spent time in the Deccan and had been influenced by its art.

Detail

## RIDER ON A NAG

**Deccan: Bijapur, mid-17th century**
Ink, opaque watercolor, and gold on paper
4 × 4⅝ in. (10 × 11.7 cm)
The Metropolitan Museum of Art, New York
Rogers Fund, 1944 (44.154)

A number of drawings from the Deccani kingdoms
that incorporate marbling are known. A whole group
of them illustrate nags; among the Sufis, nags are
thought metaphorically to embody the body's gross
desires and therefore are properly shown starved and
beaten. This salmon-and-gray horse resembles a carefully contoured piece of faux stone, its details picked
out in gold. In contrast, the ascetic rider is realized
solely in subtle shades of gray and black. Still, there is
an overall resemblance between the angular shapes of
the horse and rider, and the parallel lines of the rider's
emaciated rib cage and loincloth folds echo the nag's
faux stone striations. Thus the drawing melds its two
disparately rendered objects into a whole, the phan-
tomlike mount and its palpable rider. In conception
this extraordinary ensemble is far from both Rajput
and Mughal sensibilities, both of which strive, in quite
different ways, to achieve concreteness. Here, the
miraculous and the mystical are manifest.

## THE HOUSE OF BIJAPUR

**Deccan: Bijapur, ca. 1675**
Kamal Muhammad and Chand Muhammad
Ink, opaque watercolor, gold, and silver on paper
16¼ × 12⅛ in. (41.3 × 30.9 cm)
The Metropolitan Museum of Art, New York
Purchase, Gifts in memory of Richard Ettinghausen;
Schimmel Foundation Inc., Ehsan Yarshater, Karekin
Beshir Ltd., Margaret Mushekian, Mr. and Mrs. Edward
Ablat and Mr. and Mrs. Jerome A. Straka Gifts; The Friends
of the Islamic Department Fund; Gifts of
Mrs. A. Lincoln Scott and George Blumenthal, Bequests of
Florence L. Goldmark, Charles R. Gerth and Millie Bruhl
Frederick, and funds from various donors, by exchange;
Louis E. and Theresa S. Seley Purchase Fund for Islamic
Art and Rogers Fund, 1982 (1982.213)

From 1570 to 1685 Bijapur was the most important
center of painting in the Deccan. It was one of the last
of the Deccani kingdoms to fall to the Mughals.
Aurangzeb captured the city in 1686 and destroyed most
of the royal painting collection.[1] This marvelous painting shows the lineage of the house of Bijapur, including
the reigning sultan, gathered in a historically impossible
assemblage. The color scheme, with its dominant use of
mauve and gold as a foil to brilliant blues, reds, yellows,
warm browns, and soft greens, imparts to the picture an
otherworldly opulence. These
colors are typical of Deccani
painting. Although the careful
modeling of the faces and the
deep landscape show a relationship to naturalistic Mughal
models, the fantastic coloration
clearly departs from concerns of
naturalism, as does the emphatic
use of large-scale pattern, especially evident in the strong
arabesques of the carpet.

1. Zebrowski 1983, pp. 150, 152.

36

# DANCING DEVI, OR THE GREAT GODDESS

**Rajasthan: Bikaner, ca. 1725**
Ink, opaque and transparent watercolor, and silver on paper
21½ × 11½ in. (54.6 × 29.2 cm)
The Metropolitan Museum of Art, New York
Fletcher Fund, 1996 (1996.100.2)

This large, striking colored drawing shows the twenty-armed goddess Devi, protector of the Bikaner state, dancing on a lotus flower. Her affiliation with Shiva is made clear by both the red third eye painted on her forehead and the crescent moon to the left of her headdress. Her pleasing face, streaming hair, and beautiful clothes remind the viewer of her protective aspect; her honored position is made manifest by the silver parasol that hovers above her head. Devi's ultimate role as the avenger of cosmic disorder is expressed by the array of lethal weapons she holds, their metal rendered in silver.

The work's extraordinary vitality comes from the lyrical yet powerful rhythms of the arms, weapons, skirt, shawl, lotus leaves, and flower, silhouetted against the black ground. The rapid curve of the blunted oval surround heightens the dynamism, as does the exaggeratedly large billowing skirt with its jazzy pattern of flowers, which like some unfurling exotic bloom imparts to the goddess a colossal scale and superhuman energy.

## THE WORSHIP OF THE DEVI AS THE DARK GODDESS BHAI BHADRAKALI

**Punjab Hills: Basohli, ca. 1660–70**
Attributed to the Early Basohli Master
Page from a dispersed Tantric Devi series
Ink, opaque watercolor, gold, silver, and
beetle-wing case on paper
7 × 6⅝ in. (17.7 × 16.7 cm)
The Kronos Collections

Reference: Lerner 1984, pp. 158–63, no. 61a, ill.

The dark-skinned goddess Bhadrakali is a pacific form of the great goddess Devi. Bhadrakali is the shadow of Sati (wife of the god Shiva), who emerged after Sati committed ritual suicide because of her father's insult to Shiva. Here she stands imperiously, splendidly bejeweled, lavishly dressed, and surrounded by seven devotees. Three ferocious Kalis, emanations of the goddess who were created to kill the demon Raktabija (meaning "drop of blood"), stand to her right; they hold the demon's severed head and vessels filled with his blood, which they have collected so he cannot regenerate and multiply himself. To the goddess's left are a huge demoness called Bhima and the deity Jwala (meaning "flames of fire"). Two figures who are forms of Mahadeva (a name of Shiva) make offerings to the goddess.

The painting's scintillating color, which is embellished by raised white dots (to simulate pearls), pieces of iridescent beetle case (to mimic emeralds), silver, and gold and is enlivened by the patterns of textiles and animal skin, manifests visually the savage splendor of the goddess and her entourage. The style's bombast initially blinds us to its sophistication and artistic nuance. The drawing is refined and elegant, and the details have a palpability that stirs our senses.

### 39

## MUDITA PARAKIYA NAYIKA

**Punjab Hills: Basohli, ca. 1665**
Attributed to the Early Basohli Master
Page from a dispersed *Rasamanjari* (Essence of the
experience of delight)
Ink, opaque watercolor, gold, and beetle-wing case on paper
9⅛ × 13¼ in. (23.9 × 33.5 cm)
San Diego Museum of Art
Edwin Binney 3rd Collection (1990:1039)

This page from the earliest *Rasamanjari* series from Basohli is by the same artist as the contemporaneous Devi
series (cat. no. 38). The verse it accompanies describes
the heroine's happy anticipation of her love with the
god Krishna. All of the obstacles to their meeting are
naught: her husband lives in the cowshed, her sister-in-
law (the older woman in the palace) is blind, and the
wife of her husband's younger brother is deaf. She
stands outside the doorway to the palace and greets
Krishna.[1] The saturated colors (including the olive
green of the background), richly patterned surfaces,
flattened architecture, and profile depiction of figures
relate this painting to the Rajput pictorial tradition, as
does its traditional Hindu subject matter.

1. For the iconography, see Randhawa and Bhambri 1981, p. 38.

## 40

### RAMA VISITS HIS MOTHER BEFORE HIS EXILE

**Punjab Hills: Bahu, 1680–90**
Attributed to the Shangri Style I Master
Page from the dispersed "Shangri" *Ramayana,* Ayodhya
kanda (Story of King Rama, part 2)
Ink, opaque watercolor, and gold on paper
12½ × 8½ in. (31.6 × 21.7 cm)
Collection of Doris Wiener

The first state to embrace the Basohli style was the nearby principality of Bahu, probably under the reign of Maharaja Kripal Pal (r. 1660–90), and the earliest commission was the "Shangri" *Ramayana,* named after the location of its discovery. Several painters worked on different pages of the manuscript; this artist in particular shows close affinities with the early Basohli style and sensibility. Although the Basohli use of beetle-wing case to simulate emeralds is absent, and the drawing style is very different, the pervasive color scheme and decorative sense resemble those of the Basohli style. W. G. Archer justly employed the words "farouche, intense and frenzied" to describe this master's work.[1] His naive drawing style, coloristic and compositional exuberance, and pictorial inventiveness are informed by a sophisticated artistic sensibility, and the results are some of the most brilliant paintings in the entire Pahari (Punjab Hills) corpus.

1. Archer 1973, vol. 1, p. 326.

## 41

### THE SAGE VASISHTA VISITS RAMA

**Punjab Hills: Bahu, 1680–90**
Attributed to the Shangri Style I Master
Page from the dispersed "Shangri" *Ramayana,* Ayodhya
kanda (Story of King Rama, part 2)
Ink, opaque watercolor, and gold on paper
12½ × 8½ in. (31.6 × 21.7 cm)
Collection of Anita Spertus

In this painting Rama, an incarnation of the god Vishnu, is visited by the sage Vasishta, his spiritual preceptor, who tells him that he must purify himself for his upcoming investiture as king. The sage is shown twice, staring from both sides at the auspicious blooms of a large banana tree. The tree becomes the axis between two sequential scenes, on the right Rama eating (prior to fasting) and at left Rama with his companion, Sita, performing a *puja,* or ritual offering. Areas of brilliant saturated color, many embellished with surface patterns; exuberant forms, some of which thrust into the top margin; and layered and tilted planes that create depth in an otherwise almost flat universe are all miraculously organized into a harmonious whole. Typically, the figures are in profile, ensuring that the energy they generate remains within the picture. In a similar strategy, the Shangri Style I Master does not show sky in these *Ramayana* illustrations, limiting the degree of spatial recession. In its vitality and originality this artist's vision is as powerful and astonishing as that of the Early Basohli Master (cat. nos. 38, 39). The two painters seem to have emerged from the same cultural world.

40

41

## 42

### KING DASHARATHA AND HIS ROYAL RETINUE PROCEED TO RAMA'S WEDDING

**Punjab Hills: Bahu (Jammu), ca. 1680–90**
Perhaps by Devidasa of Nurpur
Page from the dispersed "Shangri" *Ramayana*
(Story of King Rama)
Ink and opaque watercolor on paper
8¾ × 12½ in. (22.2 × 31.8 cm)
The Metropolitan Museum of Art, New York
Purchase, The Dillon Fund, Evelyn Kranes Kossak and
Anonymous Gifts, 1994 (1994.310)

Reference: Czuma 1975, no. 110, ill.

The Shangri manuscript appears to have been abandoned in midstream with many of its pages left unfinished. They lack the final touches of gilt and polishing of the surface, which makes them appear somewhat raw when compared with contemporary images. After

Kripal Pal ceded his throne to a collateral branch of the family in 1690, his son, who retained the title but not authority to rule, did not, it seems, continue to support a painting atelier, and the artists associated with the manuscript must have moved on in search of other patronage. Pages in this style have traditionally been ascribed to an artist called the Shangri Style II Master, but in a number of significant realms—architecture, details of costume and accessories, and, most tellingly, stylized physiognomies both male and female—they seem closely related to the paintings of Devidasa of Nurpur, the artist of the Basohli *Rasamanjari* of 1694–95 (cat. no. 43). If the two painters are one and the same, the fact would conflate their rather limited separate oeuvres into a more substantial body of work. On this page, with its tumultuous procession and brilliant yellow background, details such as the spoked wheels of the carts and the types of turban also display stylistic affinities with early Basohli painting.

# SHIVA AND PARVATI PLAYING CHAUPAR

**Punjab Hills: Basohli, dated 1694–95**
Devidasa of Nurpur
Page from a dispersed *Rasamanjari* (Essence of the
experience of delight)
Ink, opaque watercolor, silver, and gold on paper
6¾ × 11 in. (17 × 28 cm)
The Metropolitan Museum of Art, New York
Gift of Dr. J. C. Burnett, 1957 (57.185.2)

Reference: Archer 1973, vol. 1, p. 46

This picture's bold conception mirrors the charged nature of the event it portrays. Shiva has just cheated his wife, Parvati, of her necklace, and she is pleading for its return. The deities sit flanking the game board on a tiger skin tilted upward toward the picture plane; on either side are trees whose pendulous heads, nodding inward, mimic the postures of the figures. Shiva, his face partially turned toward the viewer, glances slyly across the field of brilliant yellow. Although Parvati stares resolutely at her husband, the patterns of her sari, her veil, and the tiger skin tail and claws behind her betray her agitation. The forward thrust of her hand is continued by the stripes of the tiger skin, which carry our eyes back to the playful, ash-smeared god.

A clear debt to the Early Basohli Master can be seen in Shiva's face, which is similar in type to those of the Mahadeva figures on the Devi page (cat. no. 38). The brilliant coloration and bold patterning show the same ancestry. The drawing here is less subtle, however, the mood less intense, and the surface less luxuriant than their counterparts in the earlier Basohli style.

## THE GODDESS KALI SLAYING DEMONS

**Punjab Hills: Mandi, ca. 1710**
Attributed to the Mandi Master
Ink, opaque watercolor, and gold on paper
8⅛ × 11¼ in. (20.6 × 28.6 cm)
Collection of Dr. Alvin O. Bellak

Reference: Kramrisch 1986, pp. 124, 183, no. 114, ill.

Adorned with a necklace of strung heads, dressed in a skirt of severed arms, and brandishing aloft a massive sword, the horrific dark-skinned goddess stands on a pile of her demon victims. She holds up their severed heads and snarls at a retreating trio of armed demons. Her tiger steed turns toward her with a ferocity that matches her own. Only the two deer standing to the right stare at the deity without fear. They recognize the ultimate goodness of the divine avenger.

Painting from the small hill state of Mandi was always a little out of step with that of the other hill states. The extraordinarily vibrant color and patterned surface of the Basohli school never took hold there. Whereas Krishna worship prevailed throughout the hills, especially in the eighteenth century, Shiva was the deity most revered in Mandi. A number of paintings of Shivite deities by the Mandi Master survive. In this one he adopts a somewhat naive style, which helps to convey the elemental religious power of his subject.

## 45

## MAHARAJA SIDH SEN RECEIVING AN EMBASSY

**Punjab Hills: Mandi, ca. 1700–1710**
The Mandi Master
Ink and opaque watercolor on paper
14⅝ × 10⅝ in. (37 × 27 cm)
The Metropolitan Museum of Art, New York
Purchase, Florence and Herbert Irving Gift and
Rogers Fund, 1995 (1995.39)

The palette of grays, greens, and whites and the sophisticated drawing of this unusually large and ambitious painting mark it as the work of the most important Mandi painter of the early eighteenth century. The

45

maharaja and two visiting dignitaries are depicted sitting on a raised dais covered with a summer carpet while retainers and mounts stand on the ground below, a dual-level composition that derives from Mughal models. The subject and its format are unusual within the corpus of hill state painting; the picture probably records an actual meeting, one that seems filled with tension and import. In Hindu painting maharajas are often portrayed on a larger scale than their courtiers, as befits their royal state. Here the two massive figures facing each other, the white-robed Sidh Sen and his portly petitioner, have a commanding, somewhat grave presence.

## RAMA, SURROUNDED BY THE ARMIES OF THE GREAT BEAR AND MONKEY CLANS, PARDONS TWO DEMON SPIES

**Punjab Hills: Guler, ca. 1725–30**
Attributed to Manaku of Guler
Page from the dispersed Siege of Lanka series
Ink, opaque watercolor, and gold on paper
24½ × 32⅝ in. (62.2 × 82.8 cm)
The Metropolitan Museum of Art, New York
Rogers Fund, 1919 (19.24.1)

References: Craven 1990, p. 28, no. 3, ill.;
Goswamy and Fischer 1992, pp. 250–51, no. 99, ill.

Only a small number of pages from this extremely large and important series were completed. They illustrate the section of the *Ramayana* in which Rama and the bear-and-monkey army lay siege to the palace of the demon king Ravana. These paintings are among the last flowerings of a Basohli–related style to appear before a more naturalistic approach became popular in the Punjab Hills. Flat planes of undifferentiated color predominate, and color and tone are distributed with an eye to their decorative use. With great skill Manaku has knitted together visually three separate scenes from the narrative: at the upper left, Ravana commissioning the spies; in the center, the spies leaving the palace; and at right, their ultimate pardon by Rama before his assembled forces. The artist uses the light tones of the sky, the interior palace walls visible through arches, the hillock, and the three white monkeys to lead the eye from one episode to the next. The ground plane is tilted up, and the open space above the encampment makes an effective contrast to the soaring battlements of the palace.

# RAMA AND LAKSHMANA OVERWHELMED BY ARROWS

**Punjab Hills: Guler, ca. 1725–30**
Attributed to Manaku of Guler
Page from the dispersed Siege of Lanka series
Ink on paper
23½ × 33 in. (59.6 × 83.7 cm)
The Metropolitan Museum of Art, New York
Rogers Fund, 1919 (19.24.4)

Reference: Craven 1990, p. 56, no. 28, ill.

This charming, spontaneous work is a preparatory drawing, or underdrawing, for an uncompleted painting from the Siege of Lanka series. Comparing it to a finished painting in the series (cat. no. 46) is both interesting and instructive. The color applied to the paintings and the subsequent overdrawing give hardly a hint of the subtlety, variety, and psychological insight that characterize the drawings beneath. Preparatory drawings exist for several manuscripts illustrated by Manaku; this is one of two from the Siege of Lanka series in the Metropolitan Museum's collection. Rama and his brother Lakshmana have been temporarily felled by the enemies' arrows, and the animal troops surround them in dismay.

48

## THE DEMON PRALAMBA CARRIES OFF BALARAMA

**Punjab Hills: Mankot, ca. 1725**
Page from a dispersed *Bhagavata Purana* (Ancient stories
of Lord Vishnu)
Ink, opaque watercolor, and gold on paper
11⅜ × 8⅜ in. (28.9 × 21.3 cm)
Collection of Ronnie and Walter Eisenberg

This delightful page depicts a mythical game of blindman's buff during which the demon Pralamba,
momentarily disguised as a human, succeeds in fooling
the cowherds and carrying off Krishna's brother,
Balarama. (Krishna subsequently reminds his brother
that his superhuman powers are sufficient to dispatch
Pralamba with a simple knock to the head, and cosmic
order is soon restored.) With leafy tree branches the
artist has divided the composition into two sections in
which he sets the game and the abduction. With its
folksy charm, the drawing is similar in spirit to the
more inventive work of the Shangri Style I Master (see
cat. nos. 40, 41). Although the brilliant hues of the
Basohli style are still evident here, the palette is more
restricted, and while a love of overall pattern remains,
particularly apparent in the fans of foliage, the decoration is less varied and imaginative than in the earliest
versions of the style. Generally the image does not spill
over into the margin in Mankot paintings as it does in
those from Basohli and Bahu.

49

## KRISHNA SWALLOWS THE FOREST FIRE

**Punjab Hills: Basohli, ca. 1730**
Page from a dispersed *Bhagavata Purana* (?)
Ink and opaque watercolor on paper
10 × 8 in. (25.4 × 20.3 cm)
Arthur M. Sackler Museum, Harvard University
Art Museums, Cambridge
Gift of Suzanne and Frederic Weinstein in memory of
Eleanor Dodge Barton and Marjorie R. Hubbard (1991.177)

Krishna is shown swallowing a forest fire that threatened to destroy him as well as the other herders and their cattle. In earlier Pahari representations of the subject Krishna is shown with his companions in a pastoral setting, where, encircled by a ring of cows, he saves the entire company from the impending catastrophe. Here, however, he appears alone against an orange background. Shading models the face and the edges of the body, giving the figure a more three-dimensional quality than that seen in earlier Basohli works, with their emphasis on linear outline. The palette is nearly in keeping with that of earlier hill paintings, but its range is narrower. The hot orange, red, and yellow of the fire are balanced by the dusky blues of Krishna's skin and the grayish smoke. The yellow border perfectly contains and complements the image.

## 50

# SHAH JAHAN HUNTING DEER WITH TRAINED CHEETAHS

**Rajasthan: Mewar, ca. 1710**
Ink, opaque watercolor, and gold on paper
11 × 16⅝ in. (27.9 × 42.2 cm)
The Metropolitan Museum of Art, New York
Promised Gift of Cynthia Hazen Polsky

This is one of a small group of quite refined, naturalistic works done at Mewar in the beginning of the eighteenth century. Several of these depict the contemporaneous maharana Amar Singh II, but this one, curiously, commemorates a hunt that occurred in the mid-seventeenth century and has as its protagonist the Mughal emperor Shah Jahan, whose relations with the Mewari royal house had been peaceful.[1]

The picture has a gentle, lyrical quality and a mellow scheme of colors that are Mughal inspired and that soften the ferocity of the subject. The animals are beautifully observed and rendered, but the figures adhere to the stocky, somewhat wooden type that is characteristic of Mewari painting. Despite its realistic features, the scene takes place entirely in a middle ground, with no attempt to suggest spatial recession. The way the tilted ground plane is peppered with people, animals, and landscape elements owes more to traditional Rajput modes of representation than to the Mughal taste, with its penchant for direct observation.

1. By contrast, the anti-Hindu edicts of Shah Jahan's son Aurangzeb led to two years of armed conflict (1681–82) with the Rajputs, who were headed by Rana Raja Singh of Mewar.

Detail

## 51

## MAHARANA AMAR SINGH II, PRINCE SANGRAM SINGH, AND COURTIERS WATCH THE PERFORMANCE OF AN ACROBAT AND MUSICIANS

**Rajasthan: Mewar, ca. 1705–8**
Ink, opaque watercolor, and gold on paper
20½ × 35¾ in. (52.1 × 90.8 cm)
The Metropolitan Museum of Art, New York
Gift of Mr. and Mrs. Carl Bimel Jr., 1996 (1996.357)

This large, imposing painting blends the Mughal interest in reportage of actual events with a comparatively conservative Rajput aesthetic. No attempt is made to create a coherent space; the bird's-eye perspective allows the artist to distribute the pictorial elements across the page in a decorative pattern. In illustrating what seems to be a series of related events rather than a single moment, the work draws on ancient Rajput pictorial practice. A festival or fair is being celebrated. At the right the *rana* and his heir, shown arriving before a phalanx of elephants, horses, and armed soldiers, are offered trays of flowers and *pan* (a delicacy made of betel nuts). In the center a group of nobles appear to be sporting with women, while toward the left a female acrobat dances on top of a high platform to music played by a small troupe of musicians. Within a pavilion at the upper left the *rana* and his heir, flanked by four noblemen and two courtiers, sit impassively. Although they are placed toward the back of the scene, the artist has celebrated their importance by depicting them on a larger scale.

रावतकेसरीसिंधजीच

## 52

# MAHARANA JAGAT SINGH OF MEWAR HAWKING FOR CRANES

**Rajasthan: Mewar, 1744**
Shiva and Dayal
Ink, opaque watercolor, gold, and silver on paper
27 × 28¼ in. (68.6 × 73 cm)
The Metropolitan Museum of Art, New York
Fletcher Fund, 1996 (1996.100.3)

This large, complex painting is composed and colored with a freedom that is unusual—indeed, almost unprecedented. Although landscape elements are used to create a sense of specific place and to partition scenes, the whole, like the enormous sunburst that fills the top of the painting, is more fantasy than reportage. The artists have pieced together a panoramic landscape like a jigsaw puzzle; within each piece of the puzzle an episode of the hunt is portrayed. Most of the participants and animals are stock figures, but some, such as the rider being thrown from his mount in the upper left corner, are inspired and beautifully observed.

The Mewar atelier produced a great number of large-scale paintings during the eighteenth century. It was quite common for more than one artist to work on a single picture, presumably each executing a different aspect at which he was particularly skilled, such as composition, landscape features, architecture, figures, or portraits.

53

## ROYAL LOVERS (A PRINCE OFFERING WINE TO HIS MISTRESS)

**Mughal: Delhi, period of Muhammad Shah
(r. 1719–48), ca. 1740**
Ink, opaque watercolor, and gold on paper
11½ × 6¾ in. (29.3 × 17.2 cm)
San Diego Museum of Art
Edwin Binney 3rd Collection (1990:0382)

References: Binney 1973, pp. 103, 116, no. 78, ill.; Welch
1973, p. 113, no. 67, ill.; Desai 1985, p. 90, no. 72, ill.

A ripe and languorous mood pervades this fantasy
scene of amorous dalliance. Dusk is falling; a royal couple
seem spotlit against a verdant landscape beneath a red-
flecked sky. Filmy embroidered Dacca muslin veils
their brilliantly colored garments, softening the saturated hues. Although the lovers appear to stare into
each other's eyes, their glances do not meet; psychological depth has been replaced by cliché. The porce-
lain faces present an idealized perfection rather than
observation of nature. However, the exquisite rendering of the finery and the landscape generates a sense of
reality, and the polished surface offers delights to the
senses. The formulaic beauty seen in images like this
influenced both Rajasthani and Pahari painters, while
the quality of execution set the standard of royal production for much of the eighteenth century.

## 54

# MUHAMMAD SHAH ENTHRONED WITH SADAT KHAN AND HIS OFFICERS

**Mughal: Delhi, period of Muhammad Shah
(r. 1719–48), ca. 1740**

Ink, opaque watercolor, and gold on paper
12⅞ × 16⅝ in. (32.8 × 42.3 cm)
San Diego Museum of Art
Edwin Binney 3rd Collection (1990:0378)

Reference: Binney 1973, p. 103, no. 77, ill.

White becomes an important color in the Muhammad Shah period, eclipsing the brilliant hues so beloved by the Indian sensibility. Here white, green, and gold predominate. Gingerly use of the hotter colors in small touches adds richness without disturbing the painting's cool, orderly ambience. The only exception to the relentless verdure is the brilliant red of the canopy. A coherent perspective defines not only the deep space but also the huge area of the courtyard, which is nevertheless dominated by the emperor and his entourage. All the figures are formal and stiff. Works of this type had an impact on paintings of the Rajasthani, Pahari, and Company schools, affecting both their compositions and their palette.

55

## PRINCE PADAM SINGH OF BIKANER WITH HIS BARD, GORDHAR, ON A TERRACE AT NIGHT

**Rajasthan: Kishangarh, ca. 1725**
Attributed to Bhavani Das
Ink, opaque watercolor, gold, and silver on paper
11⅝ × 14 in. (29.5 × 35.6 cm)
The Metropolitan Museum of Art, New York
Promised Gift of Cynthia Hazen Polsky

Reference: Kramrisch 1986, pp. 79, 173, no. 72, ill.

The Kishangarh school of painting began in the early eighteenth century and at first was closely allied in style to contemporaneous Mughal production. The premier artist of the early period was Bhavani Das, who came from Delhi in 1719, the year of Muhammad Shah's accession, and became the most highly paid employee of the Kishangarh court. In this painting the physiognomies of the subjects are so beautifully rendered and so acutely suggestive of character that the bard's voice is almost palpable across the watery void as he recounts tales of the heroism, generosity, and religious devotion of his master. However, the sitters were not contemporaries of the artist: Padam Singh died in 1683. This is not a work of realism but a romantic evocation of the Rajasthani spirit. The terrace and landscape setting and its somber coloration derive from Mughal painting of the period, but the brilliantly colored, lavishly ornamented textiles, the decorative patterning that dominates the lower portion of the page, and the psychologically charged atmosphere are features more to a Rajput taste. Few pictures convey the pride and prowess of those great warrior princes as subtly and powerfully as this one does.

94

## LAILA AND MAJNUN CONVERSE
## BENEATH A TREE

**Rajasthan: Kishangarh, ca. 1730**
Nihal Chand
Ink, opaque watercolor, and gold on paper
12½ × 7⅜ in. (31.6 × 18.8 cm)
San Diego Museum of Art
Edwin Binney 3rd Collection (1990:0749)

The Persian story of this pair of star-crossed lovers was a popular Muslim subject of painting. Denied his beloved by his family, Majnun became an ascetic who roamed the desert and befriended the animals. In this scene he is briefly reunited with Laila.

This depiction is by another of the great artists of early Kishangarh painting, Nihal Chand. The somber palette of the deep landscape is enlivened only by Laila's brilliantly colored clothing and the bird's red head. The splendid border has fanciful hunting images drawn on a blue background with gold ink. Its form and technique derive from earlier Mughal practice, but the slithering arabesques and fantastic designs are the original work of this inspired artist. Following Mughal practice, the artist's signature is hidden in the painting, in this case on the pages of the open book between the lovers.

## A LADY PLAYING THE TANPURA

**Rajasthan: Kishangarh, ca. 1735**
Ink, opaque and transparent watercolor, and gold on paper
18½ × 13¼ in. (47 × 33.7 cm)
The Metropolitan Museum of Art, New York
Fletcher Fund, 1996 (1996.100.1)

The Kishangarh atelier is renowned not only for paintings but also for large-scale drawings that were tinted and highly finished. Images of a woman drinking wine, holding flowers, or playing an instrument became a popular genre in Rajasthani painting during the first half of the eighteenth century. They evolved from imperial Mughal depictions of large concert parties in which female entertainers served an auxiliary role. Here one such entertainer has been transformed into a *nayika*, an idealized Hindu heroine and personification of female beauty. She has just plucked a string of her *tanpura* (a drone instrument of the lute family, played by women) and is intently listening to its resonance. The drawing must date from before the 1740s, at which time a more idiosyncratic and exaggerated facial type became the vogue in Kishangarh (see cat. no. 70).

## 58

### RAJA BALWANT SINGH OF JASROTA DOES HOMAGE TO KRISHNA AND RADHA

**Punjab Hills: Jasrota, ca. 1750**
Attributed to Nainsukh of Guler
Ink, opaque watercolor, gold, and silver on paper
7¾ × 6⅛ in. (19.6 × 15.4 cm)
The Metropolitan Museum of Art, New York
Rogers Fund, 1994 (1994.377)

Little is known of Nainsukh's early life, but his painting style clearly indicates that he was aware of the art recently produced for Muhammad Shah's Mughal court. The idealized faces of Krishna and Radha in this picture are similar to those of the royal couple embracing in catalogue number 53, and the restricted palette is close to the one used by Muhammad Shah's artists. But Nainsukh, one of the greatest of Indian painters, also brings to his work qualities missing from the productions of that imperial atelier. A distinctive psycho-

logical intensity is present in the poignant figure of Balwant Singh, who meditates on and conjures up Krishna, his personal devotional deity, seated with his consort, Radha, on the maharaja's own throne.

In this painting pictorial means are perfectly wedded to intellectual intent, engendering a subtle interplay between the figures, their surroundings, and divisions of space. Balwant Singh stands at the threshold of the orange canopy, whose sweeping form defines the space containing the gods in their lavish, color-filled world. His upper body is truncated by the terrace wall; visually isolated, it is set against a desolate watery expanse. The separation between him and his vision is made all the more touching by the intervening rectangular void framed by the tent pole and the pavilion wall. But grace is manifest, not only in Krishna's gaze toward the raja but also by a pink rectangle at the base of the wall proportioned like that rectangular space, which links the throne with the void and the raja with eternity.

## KRISHNA STEALS THE BUTTER

**Punjab Hills: Basohli (?), ca. 1765**
Attributed to Nainsukh of Guler
Ink and opaque watercolor on paper
7⅛ × 11 in. (18 × 28 cm)
The Kronos Collections

Although the paintings Nainsukh made under Balwant Singh's patronage are well known, his later works are not. This late picture is unusual in his oeuvre because it is an illustration of an episode from a Hindu legend rather than a historical, allegorical, or iconic painting. Here Nainsukh combines many of his particular interests: intense psychological probing, humor, naturalism, and an almost classical ordering of the page. The scene is set on a shallow stage in front of a wall of niches housing still lifes, with the whole contained at the sides by columns and at top and bottom by architectural horizontals. The cast of characters are all absorbed in a complex psychological web of glances in which the antics of the child thief (aided by the distraction deliberately caused by his brother) are observed by everyone except his duped mother. Nainsukh integrates the restrained color and naturalistic drawing of late Mughal models with the shallow picture plane and insistent play of shapes that characterize traditional Rajput painting. The nuanced refinement of his vision only slowly unfolds to the viewer. Nainsukh's unique accomplishment makes him one of the most original and brilliant of Indian painters.

## BLINDMAN'S BUFF

**Punjab Hills: Guler, ca. 1750–55**
Manaku of Guler
Ink, opaque watercolor, and gold on paper
9⅝ × 6¾ in. (24.5 × 17.2 cm)
The Kronos Collections

References: Mehta 1926, pp. 53–54, pl. 21; Archer 1973,
vol. 1, p. 293, no. 34, and vol. 2, p. 209, ill.; Goswamy and
Fischer 1992, pp. 264–65, no. 111, ill.

This bravura painting is one of the only works by Manaku
with an inscription naming him as painter. With its extraordinary naturalistic passages, it must be one of his
last works; it heralds the great landscape paintings that
would be produced by his relatives in Kangra some
twenty years later (see cat. nos. 62–65). The artist has
brilliantly captured the look of a nighttime sky, its wispy
clouds, abundant stars, and full moon. With breathtak-
ing sureness he has rendered the moonlight caught in
the translucent leaves and blossoms and gilding the hillside. The foreground group of cows, their bodies
serenely modeled, is a marvel of observation. Although
a coherent space seems to stretch from the foreground
to the stars, a very different effect is created by the figures in the middle ground, which are unmodeled and
flat compared to the picture's other elements. Some
fleeing, some static, they appear caught by the flashbulb
of the moon; however, its illumination comes from
behind them. The hollow stare of the cows also suggests
a light source at the front of the picture. The ultimate
touch of unreality is a cow in the distance, partly
obscured by the hillside, that is identical in size and col-
or to the white cow in the foreground. The sense of
actual space is utterly negated by this device. A game is
being played in the painting not only by Krishna and
the cowherds but also between reality and illusion, the
artist and the viewer.

Detail

## 61

### AKRURA'S VISION OF VISHNU/KRISHNA

**Punjab Hills: Basohli, 1760–65**
Page from a dispersed *Bhagavata Purana* (Ancient stories of
Lord Vishnu)
Ink, opaque watercolor, and gold on paper
11½ × 16 in. (29.2 × 40.6 cm)
Philadelphia Museum of Art
Stella Kramrisch Collection (1994.148.443)

Reference: Kramrisch 1986, pp. 112, 180, no. 102, ill.

The extraordinary transformation of hill painting from
a stylized to a naturalistic art may be seen almost completed in this particularly beautiful picture. A compar-
ison with the *Bhagavata Purana* page from Mankot (cat.
no. 48) makes the progression clear: while some figures
in the later manuscript are still drawn following traditional formulas, other figures and the landscape reveal
a careful attempt to imitate nature, not only in drawing and modeling but more obviously still in the use of
color.

Two episodes are conflated into a single picture. In
the top half of the painting Akrura, a messenger of the
evil king Kamsa, the villain of the *Ramayana*, invites
Krishna and his band to come to Mathura; they set out,
drawn by horses. In the lower scene they stop on the
way, and Akrura performs his ablutions in the river.
Underwater, Krishna reveals himself as an incarnation
of Vishnu, seen seated on his serpent, Sesha, and also
shows himself in his human guise, together with his
brother. Akrura recognizes Krishna's divinity, makes
obeisance, and offers praises.

## 62

### RAMA, SITA, AND LAKSHMANA AT THE HERMITAGE OF BHARADVAJA

**Punjab Hills: Kangra, ca. 1780**
Page from a dispersed *Ramayana* (Story of King Rama)
Ink and opaque watercolor on paper
9¾ × 14 in. (24.9 × 35.7 cm)
The Metropolitan Museum of Art, New York
Rogers Fund and Seymour Fund, 1976 (1976.15)

The *Ramayana* manuscript from which this painting comes is one of the great productions of the Kangra workshop and also one of the largest in page size. Its compositions are distinguished by their variety and audacity. This one depicts the wilderness landscape into which Rama was exiled. The fantastic, tortured natural forms seem to mirror the peril and desolation felt by the god in his wanderings: a vertiginous fording of the Ganges at the upper left, the lonely valley of the hermitage at the top right, and the central hilltop scene set before an ancient windswept tree. Here Rama and his companions are seen consulting the sage Bharadvaja, who tells Rama that after his fourteen years of exile his travails are at an end and he will soon be reunited with his family.

## 63

### RADHA PINING IN THE WILDERNESS

**Punjab Hills: Kangra, ca. 1780**
Page from a dispersed *Gita Govinda* (Song of the herdsman)
Ink and opaque watercolor on paper
6½ × 10½ in. (16.5 × 26.6 cm)
Collection of Anita Spertus

A small number of paintings from this manuscript are night scenes. In them the figures are so dramatically illuminated that they appear spotlit against the dark landscape, an effect that can be traced back to painting of the Muhammad Shah period. This example is particularly effective because of the theatrical gesture made by Radha, who is shown as a *vasakasajja nayika*, a woman distraught over her absent lover. Here, in a bower beneath the stars, she waits to no avail, and her coyness turns to abandon. Her overexcited emotions are echoed by the two central trees, which display, in two different fashions, a similar sense of turbulence, and in the eddies of the river. At the upper right a messenger has been sent to Krishna, her lover, to alert him to her state. Unlike Radha, he seems totally at peace on his hillock seat.

## 64

### KRISHNA WOOS RADHA

**Punjab Hills: Kangra, ca. 1780**
Page from a dispersed *Gita Govinda* (Song of the herdsman)
Ink and opaque watercolor on paper
6¾ × 10¾ in. (17 × 27.3 cm)
The Kronos Collections

Reference: Archer 1973, vol. 1, p. 292, no. 33(iv), and
vol. 2, p. 207, ill.

In this painting an earthly seduction is used as a metaphor for the path to union with God. Krishna, the divine lover, appears four times in the picture. In the distance he is apprised of Radha's whereabouts by a messenger. In the foreground at left he encounters her, but his first advances are met guardedly and with reluctance. In the center she has melted to his caresses, while at the right she has yielded to the ecstasies of love. Thus the soul moves from not knowing to bliss. Several artists contributed to the manuscript; this page, its figures larger and its coloration lusher than those of catalogue number 63, is by a different hand. Once again nature functions both to mirror the events and to divide the pictorial space into discrete vignettes in which the tale unfolds. For example, the vine intertwined with the tree on the right, pregnant with bloom, seems to thrash like the loving couple beside it, while simultaneously it acts as a divider between the scene of dalliance and the one of lovemaking.

## 65

## THE VILLAGE BEAUTY

**Punjab Hills: Kangra, 1780**
Page from the dispersed *Bihari Sat Sai* (Seven
hundred verses)
Ink, opaque watercolor, and gold on paper
7½ × 5⅛ in. (19 × 13 cm)
The Kronos Collections

Reference: Archer 1973, vol 1, p. 296, no. 39(i), and
vol. 2, p. 214, ill.

Legend has it that the *Sat Sai* was composed by the
poet Bihari Lal for the maharaja of Amber, Jai Singh
(r. 1625–67), to entice him back to state duties after his
marriage. The book is a series of verses recounting the
loves of Krishna, which were later arranged according
to the types of *nayikas* (heroines) described. In many
cases, as here, a village setting is evoked, and the poet
dwells on a specific aspect of the woman's allure. In this
painting the blue god can be seen in the distance seated on a terrace, where an old lady is extolling the
beautiful breasts of the peasant girl in the foreground.
The artist has beautifully positioned the pictorial elements within the oval format, and the scarlets and yellows that here are synonymous with love's ardor smolder
amid the bucolic verdure.

## THE MARITAL BLISS OF NALA AND DAMAYANTI

**Punjab Hills: Kangra or Basohli, ca. 1790–1800**
Page from a dispersed *Nala-Damayanti* (Romance of Nala
and Damayanti)
Ink and watercolor on paper
11½ × 15½ in. (29.2 × 39.4 cm)
The Metropolitan Museum of Art, New York
Rogers Fund, 1918 (18.85.3)

References: Welch 1976, pp. 134–35, no. 77, ill.; Goswamy
and Fischer 1992, pp. 346–47, no. 148, ill.

In this unfinished painting the artist has made skillful
use of an elaborate architectural setting to place each
illustrated scene from the story in its own compart-
ment. All three of the buildings in the courtyard are
shown receding in perspective; closer scrutiny, however, reveals that there are three different vanishing
points. In the left-hand scene Damayanti coyly
responds to the importuning of her husband, Nala. In
the central episode, probably taking place the following day, Damayanti is urged by her handmaidens to
describe the last night's lovemaking and exhibit its
marks, while Nala tries to eavesdrop. Finally, on the
right, Nala, who walks toward a portal, is seen to have
adopted a more princely demeanor. Discrete washes of
color that have been added to the drawing begin to
articulate the large expanses and clarify the space. The
elegance and lyricism of the design are evident even
in the details, and the composition is imbued throughout with a stylized grace.

67

## A HOLI CELEBRATION

**Uttar Pradesh: Oudh, ca. 1765**
Ink and opaque watercolor on paper
18⅝ × 25 in. (47.4 × 63.5 cm)
Private collection
Courtesy of the Arthur M. Sackler Museum,
Harvard University Art Museums

References: Welch 1973, pp. 116–17, no. 69, ill.; Desai 1985,
pp. 73–74, no. 58, ill.

The first nawab (ruler) of Oudh, in East India, had been appointed governor of the province by Muhammad Shah. As the power of the Mughal court waned, this provincial court flourished and became an important center of culture.

In this painting, despite the rather raucous nature of the Holi (spring) festival, in which frolickers spray one another with brightly colored water, the nawab sits rather impassively, holding a large squirt gun. The participants, dressed in white, are seen on a white marble terrace in the foreground. A walled garden above presents a dizzying and chromatically saturated perspective view of large plots of flowers, reduced by the artist to pointillist fields of color. Although stains from colored water sully the white tonalities of the foreground, the purity of white, emphasized in works of the Muhammad Shah period, remains prominent.

68

## A CHEETAH

**Company school, 1780**
Zayn-al-din
Ink and opaque watercolor on paper
25 × 37 in. (63.5 × 94 cm)
Private collection
Courtesy of the Arthur M. Sackler Museum,
Harvard University Art Museums

Reference: Welch 1973, p. 120, no. 71a, ill.

The painter of this remarkable large-scale natural-history work, which was produced for a British patron, has filled the entire page with the image of a cheetah. The focus of the artist's attention seems to have moved restlessly: some areas convey the massing of the animal and even the texture of its fur, while the description of the hind legs and paws is abbreviated, emblematic rather than literal. The cheetah's spots take on a life of their own, becoming pure pattern. The artist has created an almost hypnotic image whose aesthetic delight lies in its exploration of decorative possibilities rather than in mimesis.

Height behind     2 - 3 3/4
Do over the shoulder   2 - 4 1/2
Length of the neck    0 - 8
Do of the body     2 - 11
Do of the tail     2 - 6
Do of the face     0 - 6 1/2
breadth of the face   0 - 6
Length of the ears    0 - 2
of the body including tail 5 - 5

چیتا

شیخ زین الدین

69

## MELANCHOLIC COURTESAN

**Rajasthan: Bundi or Kota, ca. 1750**
Ink, opaque watercolor, and gold on paper
12⅞ × 10¾ in. (32.7 × 27.3 cm)
The Metropolitan Museum of Art, New York
Purchase, Evelyn Kranes Kossak and Josephine Berger-
Nadler Gifts and funds from various donors, 1995 (1995.232)

Of the several pictures of this subject known, the
example seen here is the finest. No inscription identi-
fies the subject, but the work is probably an idealized
portrait of a courtesan. She has raised a small cup to her
lips and seems lost in reverie. Her melancholy may be
due simply to alcohol, but more likely she was associated with a particular story that has not come down to
us. Her upper body is nude; she has bedecked herself

with jewels and is awaiting a customer. Although courtesans are not traditionally associated with romantic
love, they are named as one of the basic types of *nayika*
(heroine), Sadharani or Samanya *nayika*. The practice of
depicting courtesans came from Persia into the artistic
repertoire of Muslim India and thence to Hindu painting. This compositional formula, with a textile hung
over a window ledge in the foreground and behind it
the subject set against a green background, derives from
Mughal prototypes. In all other respects, however, the
work is purely Rajput. Large areas of undifferentiated
color modeled with black make up the textiles, all
elaborately patterned in gold, and the heroine's flesh.
The extraordinarily subtle modeling and the delicacy of
the picture's execution throughout are typical of some
Bundi-Kota painting of the period.

## 70

### KRISHNA AND RADHA LIE IN A BOWER

**Rajasthan: Kishangarh, ca. 1750**
Attributed to Nihal Chand
Ink, opaque watercolor, and gold on paper
8¼ × 12¼ in. (22.2 × 31.2 cm)
San Diego Museum of Art
Edwin Binney 3rd Collection (1990:0756)

Reference: Welch 1973, pp. 58–59, no. 29, ill.

The mood of this devotional painting, both languorous and auspicious, is created by the dense, verdant forest setting and the mannered depiction of the nestled lovers and attending *gopis* (cowherds). The verisimilitude of the early Kishangarh style has evolved here toward a more metaphoric rendering of the world in which scale is discontinuous, space is shallower, and figures are idealized; a more traditional Rajput sensibility has reasserted itself. The exaggerated facial type is thought to derive from the features of the courtesan Bani Thani, who became the consort of Kishangarh's Maharaja Nagari Das and the inspiration for poetry he wrote celebrating the love of Radha and Krishna.

## 71

## KRISHNA AND THE GOPIS TAKE SHELTER FROM THE RAIN

**Rajasthan: Jaipur, ca. 1760**
Ink, opaque watercolor, and gold on paper
13¾ × 9⅜ in. (34.9 × 23.8 cm)
The Metropolitan Museum of Art, New York
Purchase, Mr. and Mrs. John E. Wiley and Cynthia Hazen
Polsky Gifts, and Rogers Fund, 1991 (1991.94)

This large picture is remarkable for its representation of an acutely observed landscape in which flora and fauna are rendered with almost obsessive detail. Some of the figures are on the same scale as the landscape, but others, especially those of Krishna and Radha, are disproportionately large, defying the natural rules of spatial recession. In Indian painting, shifts in scale of this type are sometimes used, as here, to signify differences in rank. In this instance the effect is somewhat fantastic, and that impression is reinforced by the excessively small cows in the foreground. The artist is most adept at profiles, as is often the case in Hindu painting. Here, the slightly distorted three-quarter-view faces add a rather naive touch to the work.

The painting alludes to a legend in which Krishna held Mount Govardhan up as a shield to save the world from a torrential rain sent by the god Indra. In this painting a cloak suffices to convey the meaning.

Detail

## 72

## MAHARANA ARI SINGH WITH HIS COURTIERS AT THE JAGNIWAS WATER PALACE

**Rajasthan: Mewar, 1767**
Bhima, Kesu Ram, Bhopa, and Nathu
Ink, opaque watercolor, gold, and silver on paper
26¼ × 33 in. (67.9 × 83.8 cm)
The Metropolitan Museum of Art, New York
Purchase, Mr. and Mrs. Herbert Irving, Mr. and Mrs.
Arthur Ochs Sulzberger, and Mr. and Mrs. Henry A.
Grunwald Gifts, in honor of Mr. and Mrs. Gustavo
Cisneros, 1994 (1994.116)

This is one of the finest and largest paintings from the period of the maharana Ari Singh (r. 1761–73). It shows the maharana and his assembled courtiers seated in a pavilion, below which a dance entertainment is taking place. Like many Mewari pictures it combines multiple perspectives, permitting the artist to reveal elements of the scene that would otherwise be hidden. Thus, the left-hand courtyard wing of the palace has been rotated counterclockwise to display the exterior of the walls and to make visible the garden retreat of the maharana, who appears several times in the painting. In the central scene a kind of reverse perspective is employed in which the sight lines diverge and figures increase in size as they recede in space. A predominant monochrome established by the silver water, white marble palace, and black-and-white checkerboard floor is enlivened by saturated colors in the textiles of clothing and decor and by the greens of the garden room. The simplicity of the color scheme recalls early Rajasthani painting. Although four artists worked on this picture, Bhima appears to have been the principal author.

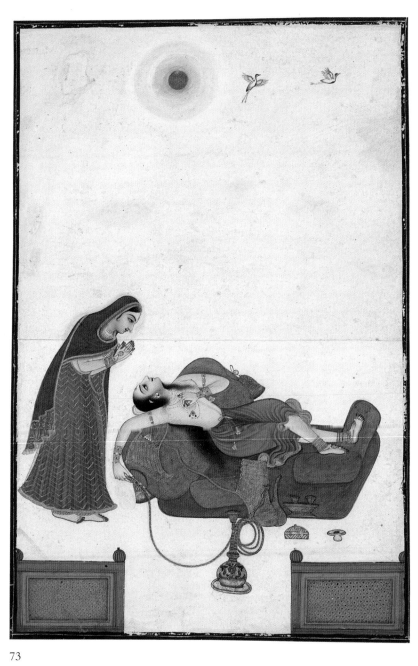

73

## LADY YEARNING FOR HER LOVER

**Rajasthan: Bundi, ca. 1780**
Ink, opaque watercolor, and gold on paper
9¾ × 6¾ in. (24.4 × 16.2 cm)
Arthur M. Sackler Museum, Harvard University
Art Museums, Cambridge
Gift of John Kenneth Galbraith

On a marble terrace by the light of a full moon, a lady intoxicated from smoking her hookah languishes on a bed of cushions, yearning for her beloved. She stares into space, insensible of the attendant who bends over her in concern and with hands raised in a gesture of respect. The lovesick woman's inner agitation is made palpable by the rhythmic folds and undulating hemlines of her green skirt and diaphanous scarf. Her body is torpid; the pale skin of her naked upper body is accentuated by her long black hair. The contained energy of the figures is played against the huge white void of terrace and sky, in which the sole elements are a ringed moon and two lone birds, one winging toward its coasting mate. The composition is anchored by the two parapet walls at the bottom. This work is one of the most evocative of Rajasthani paintings, quintessentially Indian in its ability to make an emotional state visible and palpable.

## SINGER AND SARANGI PLAYER

**Rajasthan: Jaipur, ca. 1800**
Attributed to Sahib Ram
Cartoon for a mural depicting the Rasalila (Circle dance of Krishna and the *gopis*)
Ink on paper
20¼ × 20 in. (51.4 × 50.8 cm)
The Metropolitan Museum of Art, New York
Rogers Fund, 1918 (18.85.4)

Reference: Coomaraswamy 1916, pl. x

## HEAD OF KRISHNA

**Rajasthan: Jaipur, ca. 1800**
Attributed to Sahib Ram
Cartoon for a mural depicting the Rasalila (Circle dance of Krishna and the *gopis*)
Ink and watercolor on paper
27¼ × 18½ in. (69.2 × 47 cm)
The Metropolitan Museum of Art, New York
Rogers Fund, 1918 (18.85.2)

Reference: Coomaraswamy 1916, pl. ix

As it had been in the preceding century, painting in Amber/Jaipur during the eighteenth century continued to be heavily influenced by Mughal aesthetics, and many of the artists employed at the court were Muslims. (The state previously called Amber has been known as Jaipur ever since its new capital city of that name was founded in 1727 by Jai Singh II.) Comparatively few paintings from Jaipur are in Western collections because the royal collection, unlike those of many other Rajasthani courts, was never dispersed. Maharaja Sawai Pratap Singh, who came to the throne in 1784, was a great patron of art whose atelier housed more than twenty artists.[1] Perhaps the finest painter was Sahib Ram, a Muslim active at Jaipur throughout the second half of the eighteenth century. His masterpiece was a mural painting of Radha and Krishna dancing, for which the two drawings catalogue numbers 74 and 75 are preparatory studies. Murals had adorned Indian buildings beginning at least in the Mughal period, although most are now lost or inaccessible for viewing. These two drawings, which were pricked, probably to allow their images to be transferred to the palace wall, are a reminder of an important category of Indian painting otherwise unrepresented in this catalogue.

1. Das n.d., pp. 77–94.

74

75

76

## A TIGER HUNT

**Rajasthan: Kota, 1780 (dated: Samvat 1837)**
Sheikh Taju
Ink and transparent watercolor on paper
11⅝ × 27⅜ in. (29.5 × 69.5 cm)
The Metropolitan Museum of Art, New York
Promised Gift of Cynthia Hazen Polsky

Reference: Hodgkin and McInerney 1983, no. 35, ill.

In the center a maharaja, barely visible on his treetop platform, is aiming at a ferocious tiger, who snarls at him from a dense forest set before rocky cliffs. This sheet is the top half of a study for an important painting presently in the collection of the maharaja of Jodhpur. The bottom half of the study is in the Jagdish and Kamla Mittal Museum of Indian Art in Hyderabad. Only a few works bear the signature of Sheikh Taju, who is now thought to be the creator of some of the most famous Kota paintings of the second half of the eighteenth century.[1]

This study is unusual for its painterly quality. The feathery drawing is supplemented by notations of colors as well as by large areas of blocked-in color; other portions that have been strengthened with black ink become almost calligraphic in their clarity. The execution is varied, fresh, and immediate, and the effect is of a quite unique modernity.

1. Stuart Cary Welch, personal communication.

## 77

### A PRINCE HUNTING BOARS WITH HIS RETINUE

**Rajasthan: Jhilai, late 18th–early 19th century**
Ink, opaque watercolor, and gold on paper
11⅛ × 15⅞ in. (28.4 × 40.3 cm)
The Metropolitan Museum of Art, New York
Fletcher Fund, 1996 (1996.100.4)

Jhilai, a feudatory state of Jaipur, was small but important, since its rulers were next in succession to the throne of Jaipur if the main line proved without issue. In the late eighteenth and early nineteenth centuries a significant but little-known style of painting seems to have flourished in Jhilai, probably representing the work of a single artist. This painting is perhaps the finest of his known works. The strong colors favored by the Jaipur school are here tempered into sober fields of black, gray, and green, and the classical balance typical of that school gives way to a more mannered treatment. The Jhilai artist has created a dynamic composition of taut forms and bold surface patterns; its elements, both distant and close, are described with crystalline clarity. The breadth and geometric severity of the extraordinarily large lake palace act as a foil for the staccato rhythms of the troop of hunters.

## MAHARANA BHIM SINGH OF MEWAR AND HIS RETINUE GOING TO A HUNT

**Rajasthan: Mewar or Devgarh, ca. 1805–10**
Attributed to Chokha
Ink, opaque watercolor, and gold on paper
15 × 16¼ in. (38.1 × 41 cm)
The Metropolitan Museum of Art, New York
Fletcher Fund, 1996 (1996.100.5)

In the last quarter of the eighteenth century a new school of painting began to flourish in Devgarh, a feudatory state of Mewar. Court painters of four generations are known, the last three of whom were relat-ed: Bakta, his son Chokha, and his son, Baijnath. As at Mewar, a dominant Rajput artistic sensibility is apparent in the use of strong primary colors, dense rhythmic patterns, and bursting forms. Hunting and *darbar* scenes predominate. The fort at Devgarh is one of the few in which frescoes survive from the late eighteenth and early nineteenth centuries. They show that the same court artists who made portable paintings also worked on large-scale building decorations.[1]

Chokha produced paintings for the Mewar court as well as the Devgarh court, making the precise localization of his paintings difficult.

1. Beach 1970–71.

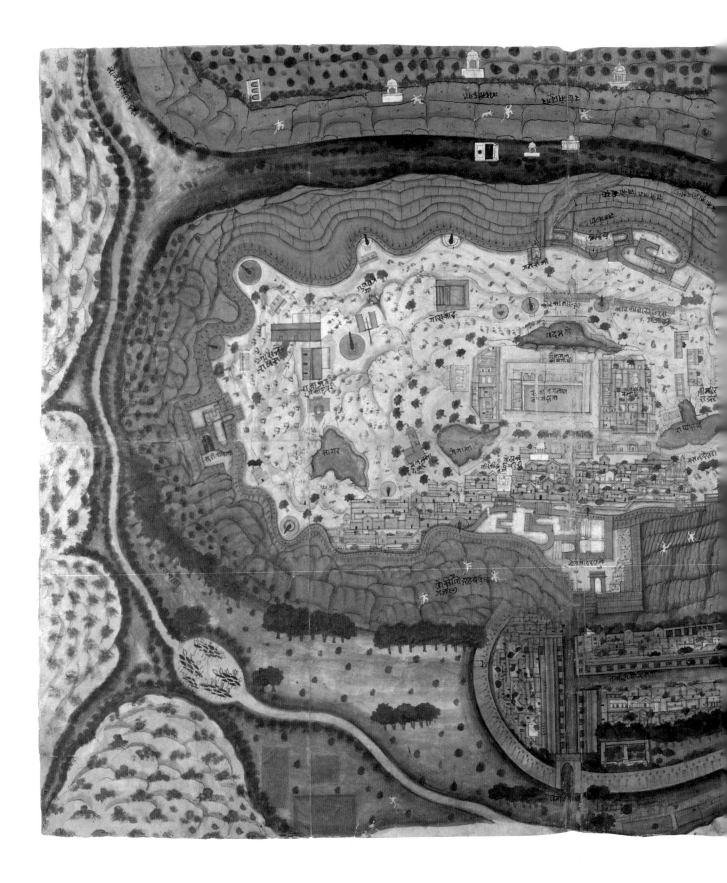

## THE CITY AND HILL FORTRESS
## OF RANTHAMBHOR

**Rajasthan: Jaipur, early 19th century**
Ink and opaque watercolor on paper
29 × 40¼ in. (73.7 × 102.2 cm)
The Metropolitan Museum of Art, New York
Fletcher Fund, 1996 (1996.100.6)

The tenth-century fort of Ranthambhor, set on a tall, isolated crag in a heavily forested area between Jaipur and Kota and now in ruins, is one of the most famous and forbidding structures in India. In the early nineteenth century it was used by Maharaja Jagat Singh of Jaipur (r. 1803–18), who is mentioned in one of the many inscriptions on this painting. The work can be dated to his reign. Although the main view is aerial, individual elements are treated in oblique perspective, making them easily identifiable. Simultaneously a topographical study and a map, this compelling painting transcends both categories. The artist has created an image with almost organic overtones, in which the recorded facts are subsumed by his pictorial inventiveness and turned into a grand design.

## THE MARRIAGE CELEBRATIONS AT UDAIPUR OF MAHARAO RAM SINGH II OF KOTA

**Rajasthan: Kota, ca. 1851**
Ink, opaque watercolor, and gold on cotton
36½ × 27¼ in. (92.6 × 69.5 cm)
Collection of Howard Hodgkin

Reference: Topsfield and Beach 1991, pp. 108–9, no. 42, ill.

It is interesting to note the prominence in this painting of armed British troops, escorting a palanquin whose occupant is not, however, granted the distinction of being portrayed. Ram Singh II was one of the last great Rajput patrons. In a situation of British dominance and the decline of his own political circumstances, he turned his energies to amusements, festivals, and the arts. He married the sister of Sarup Singh of Udaipur on March 9, 1851; this painting by a Kota artist commemorates the reception with which the maharana welcomed him to Udaipur. The painting shows similarities to late-eighteenth-century Mewari pictures but is more realistic, both in the characterization of individuals and in the truer perspectival description of architecture. Even so, as in the earlier works, objects do not diminish in size as they recede, and the most significant personages are painted on a larger scale. The restricted color range harks back to the fundamental color scheme of Indian art. The composition of the picture is exuberant and original, its forms and colors arranged with an almost abstract sensibility.

Detail

# A SYCE HOLDING TWO CARRIAGE HORSES

**Company school, Calcutta, mid-19th century**
Shaykh Muhammad Amir of Karraya
Ink and opaque watercolor on paper
12 × 20 in. (30.5 × 50.8 cm)
The Metropolitan Museum of Art, New York
Louis E. and Theresa S. Seley Purchase Fund for Islamic Art and
Rogers Fund, 1994 (1994.280)

There is something hypnotic and disquieting about this near mirror image of a *syce,* or groom, flanked by almost identical horses. The artist has chosen a pictorial format whose power is as decorative as it is descriptive. The strict symmetry is relieved, however, by subtle differences in the horses' sizes, proportions, and harnessing, as well as by slight left-right variations in the posture and dress of the groom. The darks are very dark and the lights very light, intensifying the decorative appeal of the composition. Although the color is severely restricted, the artist has beautifully realized the feel of Indian light, and the low horizon line makes both the space and the foreground trio appear truly monumental. This painting's beauty and subtlety testify to the high quality that late Company school artists could attain.

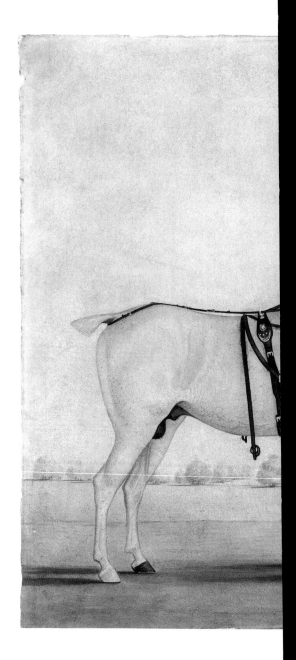

82

## MAHARAJA SARDAR SINGH OF BIKANER

**Rajasthan: Bikaner, ca. 1860–70**
Chotu
Ink, opaque watercolor, and gold on paper
16 × 12 in. (40.6 × 30.5 cm)
The Metropolitan Museum of Art, New York
Fletcher Fund, 1996 (1996.100.7)

Maharaja Sardar Singh (r. 1851–72) is captured here in an extraordinary portrait whose painter was undoubtedly aware of the inroads photography was making among royal patrons. The painting exhibits what at first glance seems an almost photographic realism. However, Chotu has carefully manipulated the picture's elements to play two- and three-dimensional forms off against each other, achieving an almost surreal effect. Note particularly how the lower edge of the beard continues the line of the cushion and how the outlines of cushion, beard, shoulders, and window frame con-

83

verge, making the maharaja's head appear to float before the gray rectangle of the window. The unearthly quality is heightened by the composition's commanding symmetry, even down to the cleft beard and the bosses on the shield. The dominant vertical axis is balanced by strong horizontals. A few asymmetrical elements offset the regularity, including the pleated shawl and garment and the fantastical turban, which is like some postmodern assemblage crowning the brooding visage.

## 83

### TANTRIC FORM OF PARAMA SHIVA

**Rajasthan: Jaipur (?), 19th century**
Ink, opaque watercolor, gold, and silver on paper
9⅛ × 6½ in. (23.2 × 16.5 cm)
Collection of Helen Marden

The imagery of this painting seems to refer to Kundalini yoga, in which the practitioner attempts progressively to elevate energy along his own body's *chakras* (energy centers) to the highest one in his cranium, in order to reach a state of divinity that is identified with Parama Shiva and is understood to be the union of Shiva and Shakti (female energy). The body's energy is visualized as a snake, and the experience of inner divinity is expressed as the opening of a thousand-petaled lotus. Here Shiva's body is composed of a male and a female body in sexual union, seen in profile, their limbs twined with cobras. The cobras' heads emerge to flank the head of the god, which is topped by his abode, Mount Kailasa, and encircled by a lotus-flower aureole. With its brilliant coloration, quirky style, and sexualized subject matter, this painting is evocative and powerful.

# SELECTED BIBLIOGRAPHY

**Archer, W. G.**

1973     *Indian Paintings from the Punjab Hills: A Survey and History of Pahari Miniature Painting.* 2 vols. London.

**Banerjee, Anil Chandra**

1983     *Aspects of Rajput State and Society.* New Delhi.

**Beach, Milo Cleveland**

1970–71     "Painting at Devgarh." *Archives of Asian Art* 24, pp. 23–35.

1974     *Rajput Painting at Bundi and Kota.* Ascona, Switz.

1978     *The Grand Mogul: Imperial Painting in India.* Exh. cat. Williamstown, Mass.: Sterling and Francine Clark Art Institute.

1981     *The Imperial Image: Paintings for the Mughal Court.* Exh. cat. Washington, D.C.: Freer Gallery of Art.

1992     *Mughal and Rajput Painting.* Vol. 1, pt. 3 of *The New Cambridge History of India.* Cambridge.

**Binney, Edwin, 3rd**

1973     *Indian Miniature Painting from the Collection of Edwin Binney 3rd.* Vol. 1, *The Mughal and Deccani Schools, with Some Related Sultanate Material.* Exh. cat. Portland, Oreg.: Portland Art Museum.

**Binney, Edwin, 3rd, and W. G. Archer**

1968     *Rajput Miniatures from the Collection of Edwin Binney 3rd.* Exh. cat. Portland, Oreg.: Portland Art Museum.

**Brown, Percy**

1924     *Indian Painting under the Mughals, A.D. 1550 to A.D. 1750.* Oxford. Reprint, New Delhi, 1981.

**Cimino, Rosa Maria**

1985     *Vita di corte nel Rajasthan: Miniature indiane dal XVII al XIX secolo.* Exh. cat. Turin: Palazzo Reale.

**Coomaraswamy, Ananda K.**

1916     *Rajput Painting; Being an Account of the Hindu Paintings of Rajasthan and the Panjab Himalayas from the Sixteenth to the Nineteenth Century, Described in Their Relation to Contemporary Thought. . . . 2 vols. London.*

**Craven, Roy C., Jr., ed.**

1990     *Ramayana: Pahari Paintings.* Bombay.

**Czuma, Stanislaw**

1975     *Indian Art from the George P. Bickford Collection.* Exh. cat. Cleveland: Cleveland Museum of Art.

**Das, Asok Kumar**

n.d.     "Miniatures." In *Homage to Jaipur,* pp. 77–94, 102. Bombay.

**Desai, Vishaka N.**

1985     *Life at Court: Art for India's Rulers, 16th–19th Centuries.* Exh. cat. Boston: Museum of Fine Arts.

1990     "Painting and Politics in Seventeenth Century North India, Mewar, Bikaner, and the Mughal Court." *Art Journal* 49, no. 4 (Winter), pp. 370–78.

**Dickson, Martin Bernard, and Stuart Cary Welch**

1981     *The Houghton Shahnameh.* 2 vols. Cambridge, Mass.

**Dimand, Maurice S.**

1948     "Several Illustrations from the Dastan-i Amir Hamza in American Collections." *Artibus Asiae* 11, pp. 5–13.

**Gascoigne, Bamber**

1971     *The Great Moghuls.* New York.

**Glynn, Catherine**

1983     "Early Painting in Mandi." *Artibus Asiae* 44, pp. 21–64.

1996     "Evidence of Royal Painting for the Amber Court." *Artibus Asiae* 56, pp. 67–93.

**Goswamy, B. N., and Eberhard Fischer**

1992     *Pahari Masters: Court Painters of Northern India. Artibus Asiae*, suppl. 38. Zurich.

**Hodgkin, Howard, and Terence McInerney**

1983     *Indian Drawing.* Exh. cat. London: Arts Council of Great Britain.

**Hutchins, Francis G., trans.**

1980     *Young Krishna.* West Franklin, N.H.

**Kramrisch, Stella**

1986     *Painted Delight: Indian Paintings from Philadelphia Collections.* Exh. cat. Philadelphia: Philadelphia Museum of Art.

**Lerner, Martin**

1984     *The Flame and the Lotus: Indian and Southeast Asian Art from The Kronos Collection.* Exh. cat. New York: The Metropolitan Museum of Art.

**Lukens, Marie G.**

1965     *Guide to the Collections: Islamic Art.* New York: The Metropolitan Museum of Art.

**Mehta, Nanalal Chamanlal**

1926     *Studies in Indian Painting: A Survey of Some New Material Ranging from the Commencement of the VIIth Century to circa 1870 A.D.* Bombay.

**Punjab States Gazetteers**

1910     *Punjab States Gazetteers.* Vol. 22A, *Chamba State, with Maps, 1904.* Lahore.

**Randhawa, Mohindra Sinh, and S. D. Bhambri**

1981     *Basohli Paintings of the Rasamanjari.* New Delhi.

**Randhawa, Mohindra Sinh, and John Kenneth Galbraith**

1968     *Indian Painting: The Scene, Themes, and Legends.* Boston.

**Randhawa, Mohindra Sinh, and Doris Schreier Randhawa**

1980     *Kishangarh Painting.* Bombay.

**Tod, James**

1920     *Annals and Antiquities of Rajasthan or the Central and Western Rajput States of India.* 3 vols. London.

**Topsfield, Andrew**

1980     *Paintings from Rajasthan in the National Gallery of Victoria: A Collection Acquired through the Felton Bequests' Committee.* Melbourne.

1984     *An Introduction to Indian Court Painting.* London.

**Topsfield, Andrew, and Milo Cleveland Beach**

1991     *Indian Paintings and Drawings from the Collection of Howard Hodgkin.* New York.

**Welch, Stuart Cary**

1973     *A Flower from Every Meadow: Indian Paintings from American Collections.* Exh. cat. New York: Asia House Gallery.

1976     *Indian Drawings and Painted Sketches, 16th through 19th Centuries.* Exh. cat. New York: Asia House Gallery.

1978     *Imperial Mughal Painting.* New York.

1983     "Return to Kotah." In *Essays on Near Eastern Art and Archaeology in Honor of Charles Kyrle Wilkinson,* edited by Prudence O. Harper and Holly Pittman, pp. 78–93. New York: The Metropolitan Museum of Art.

1984     *India: Art and Culture, 1300–1900.* Exh. cat. New York: The Metropolitan Museum of Art.

1995     "The Two Worlds of Payag—Further Evidence on a Mughal Artist." In *Indian Art and Connoisseurship: Essays in Honor of Douglas Barrett,* edited by John Guy, pp. 320–41. Middleton, N.J.

**Welch, Stuart Cary, and Milo Cleveland Beach**

1965     *Gods, Thrones, and Peacocks: Northern Indian Painting from Two Traditions, Fifteenth to Nineteenth Centuries.* Exh. cat. New York: Asia House Gallery. Reprint, New York, 1976.

**Welch, Stuart Cary, Annemarie Schimmel, Marie L. Swietochowski, and Wheeler M. Thackston**

1987     *The Emperors' Album: Images of Mughal India.* Exh. cat. New York: The Metropolitan Museum of Art.

**Zebrowski, Mark**

1983     *Deccani Painting.* London.

# LENDERS TO THE EXHIBITION

*Numbers cited refer to catalogue entries.*

Dr. Alvin O. Bellak: 28, 44

Ronnie and Walter Eisenberg: 48

Howard Hodgkin: 19, 30, 80

The Knellington Collection: 29

The Kronos Collections: 17, 32, 38, 59, 60, 64, 65

Helen Marden: 83

Philadelphia Museum of Art: 61

Arthur M. Sackler Museum, Harvard University Art Museums, Cambridge: 49, 73

San Diego Museum of Art: 14, 39, 53, 54, 56, 70

Anita Spertus: 3, 6, 16, 41, 63

Stuart Cary Welch: 31

Doris Wiener: 40

Anonymous lenders: 23, 27, 67, 68

All other works are in the collections of The Metropolitan Museum of Art, New York.

# INDEX

*Page references to illustrations are in italics.*

Abd-as-Samad, 9

Abu'l Hasan, 12

Akbar, 9–13, 36, 38, 40, *40–41*, 43, 49,
    51, 52
    Fatehpur Sikri style during rule of,
        9–10, 32, *33*, 34, *34–35*
    Lahore style during rule of, 10, 12, 38,
        *38*, 39, *39*, 40, *40–41*
    *See also* Mughal style, Akbar period
*Akbar-nama* (Chronicle of Akbar), 10, 40,
    *40, 41*; cat. no. 13

Akrura, 102, *102*

Amar Singh II, Maharana, 86, 88, *88–89*

Amber (Rajasthan), 10, 11–12, 43
    *Krishna Fluting* (Boston *Rasikapriya*),
        12, 43, *43*; cat. no. 15

Amber-Jaipur area style, 119

Amir Khosrow Dihlavi, *Hasht Behesht*
    (Eight Paradises), 10, 39, *39*

Anup Singh, 17

Ari Singh, Maharana, *2*, 116, *116–17*

Assad Ibn Kariba, 34, *34–35*

Aurangzeb, 14–15, 17, 18, 53, 57, *57*, 64,
    68. *See also* Mughal style,
        Aurangzeb period

Azam, 57, *57*

Babur, 9, 48

Bahram Gur, *11*, 39, *39*

Bahu (Jammu) (Punjab Hills), 19, 74, 84
    *King Dasharatha and His Royal Retinue
        Proceed to Rama's Wedding*
        (Shangri *Ramayana*) (Devidasa
        of Nurpur [?]), 19, 76, *76*;
        cat. no. 42
    *Rama Visits His Mother Before His Exile*
        (Shangri *Ramayana*) (attrib.
        Shangri Style I Master), 19,
        74, *75*, 84; cat. no. 40
    *The Sage Vasishta Visits Rama* (Shangri
        *Ramayana*) (attrib. Shangri
        Style I Master), 19, 74, 75, 84;
        cat. no. 41

Baijnath, 125

Bakta, 125

Balarama, 31, *31*, 38, *38*, 84, *84*

Balwant Singh, Raja, of Jasrota, 21–22,
    98, *98*

Banaras, 14

Bani Thani, 21, 113

Basohli (Punjab Hills), 18–19, 21, 22, 73,
    74, 76, 77, 78, 84, 85, 107
    *Akrura's Vision of Vishnu/Krishna* (*Bha-
        gavata Purana*), 102, *102*; cat.
        no. 61
    *Krishna Swallows the Forest Fire* (*Bhagavata
        Purana*), 19, 85, *85*; cat. no. 49
    *Mudita Parakiya Nayika* (*Rasamanjari*)
        (attrib. Early Basohli Master),
        19, 73, *73*, 74; cat. no. 39
    *Shiva and Parvati Playing Chaupar*
        (*Rasamanjari*) (Devidasa of
        Nurpur), 19, 76, 77, *77*; cat.
        no. 43
    *The Worship of the Devi as the Dark
        Goddess Bhai Bhadrakali*
        (Tantric Devi series) (attrib.
        Early Basohli Master), 18, 72,
        *72*, 73, 74, 77; cat. no. 38

Basohli (?), *Krishna Steals the Butter*
    (attrib. Nainsukh of Guler), 22,
    99, *99*; cat. no. 59

Basohli or Kangra. *See* Kangra or Basohli

Basohli-related style, 80

Bengal school, Pala period, *Pancavimsati-
    sahasrika Prajnaparamita*, 6, *6*; fig. 3

Bhadrakali, 72

*Bhagavata Purana* (Ancient stories of Lord
    Vishnu), 7, *8*, 19, 27, *27*, 28, *28*,
    29, *29*, 30, 38, 47, 84, *84*, 85, *85*,
    102, *102*; cat. nos. 2, 3, 4, 48, 49,
    61; fig. 4
    Isarda manuscript, 7, 27, 30, *30*, 31, *31*;
        cat. nos. 5, 6

Bhai Bhadrakali (Devi as the Dark God-
    dess), 72, *72*

Bharadvaja, 103

Bhavani (goddess), 52

Bhavani Das, 21, 94

Bhavani Das (attrib.), *Prince Padam Singh
    of Bikaner with his Bard, Gordhar,
    on a Terrace at Night*, 21, 94, *94*;
    cat. no. 55

Bhima (demoness), 72, *72*

Bhima, Kesu Ram, Bhopa, and Nathu,
    *Maharana Ari Singh with His*

*Courtiers at the Jagnivas Water Palace*,
    *2*, 22, 116, *116–17*; cat. no. 72; fig. 1

Bhim Singh, Maharana, of Mewar, 125, *125*

Bhoj Singh, Rao, of Bundi, 62–63, *63*

Bihari Lal, 106

*Bihari Sat Sai* (Seven hundred verses), 22,
    100, 106, *106*; cat. no. 65

Bijapur (Deccan), 15, 68
    *The House of Bijapur* (Kamal Muham-
        mad and Chand Muham-
        mad), 15, 68, *69*; cat. no. 36
    *Rider on a Nag*, 15, 68, *68*; cat. no. 35

Bikaner (Rajasthan), 10, 11–12, 15, 17,
    18, 23, 66
    *Dancing Devi, or The Great Goddess*, 70,
        *71*; cat. no. 37
    *Kedar Ragini* (*Ragamala* series)
        (Ruknuddin), 17, 65, *65*; cat.
        no. 33
    *Ladies on a Terrace* (Ruknuddin), 15, *16*,
        17, 64, *64*, 65; cat. no. 32; fig. 7
    *Maharaja Sardar Singh of Bikaner* (Chotu),
        132–33, *132*; cat. no. 82
    *Panchama Ragini* (*Ragamala* series), 12,
        17, 46, *46*; cat. no. 18

Bikaner or the Deccan, *Demons Fighting
    Over an Animal Limb*, 17, 66, *66*,
    *67*; cat. no. 34

Bilaspur, 19

Brahma, 28, *28*, 42, *42*

British, 23. *See also* Company school

Buddhist manuscripts, illustrated, 4–6, *6*

Bulaqi, *Shah Jahan Watching an Elephant
    Fight* (*Padshah-nama*), 14, 53, 55,
    61; cat. no. 25

Bundi (Rajasthan), 12, 15, 17–18, 23, 45
    *Lady Yearning for Her Lover*, 22, 118, 119;
        cat. no. 73
    *Rao Raton of Bundi*, 18, 58, *58*; cat. no. 28
    *A Royal Horse with His Groom*, 12, 45,
        *45*; cat. no. 17

Bundi-Kota style, 63, 112

Bundi or Kota (Rajasthan), *Melancholic
    Courtesan*, 22, 112, *112*; cat. no. 69

Calcutta (Company school), *A Syce
    Holding Two Carriage Horses*
    (Shaykh Muhammad Amir of
    Karraya), 130, *130–31*; cat. no. 81

Chamba, 19, 22

*Chaurapanchasika* (Fifty stanzas of secret love), 7

*Chaurapanchasika* style, 7, *8*, 10, 30, 44

   *Brahma Prostrates Himself Before Krishna* (*Bhagavata Purana*), 7, 28, *28*, 30; cat. no. 3

   *The Gopis Beseech Krishna to Return Their Clothing* (Isarda *Bhagavata Purana*), 7, 27, 30, *30*; cat. no. 5

   *Krishna Battles the Armies of the Demon Naraka* (*Bhagavata Purana*), 7, *8*, 29, *29*, 30; cat. no. 4; fig. 4

   *Krishna Kills the Evil King Kamsa's Washerman* (Isarda *Bhagavata Purana*), 7, 27, 31, *31*; cat. no. 6

   *Nanda and Vasudeva* (*Bhagavata Purana*), 7, 27, *27*, 28, 30; cat. no. 2

Chitarman, *Shah Jahan on a Terrace Holding a Pendant Set with His Portrait* (leaf from album for Shah Jahan), 13, *13*, 14, 53, *54*; cat. no. 24; fig. 6

Chokha, 125

Chokha (attrib.), *Maharana Bhim Singh of Mewar and His Retinue Going to a Hunt*, 23, 125, *125*; cat. no. 78

Chotu, 132

   *Maharaja Sardar Singh of Bikaner*, 132–33, *132*; cat. no. 82

Company school, 23, 93, 130

   *A Cheetah* (Zayn-al-din), 23, 109, *110–11*; cat. no. 68

   *A Syce Holding Two Carriage Horses* (Shaykh Muhammad Amir of Karraya), 130, *130–31*; cat. no. 81

Damayanti, 107, *107*

Dara Shikoh, 14, 18, 49, *50*

Dasharatha, King, 76, *76*

Deccan, 3, 14, 15, 17, 22, 63, 66, 68. *See also* Bijapur; Bikaner or the Deccan

Delhi (period of Shah Jahan), 3, 12, 20, 22

   *Muhammad Shah Enthroned with Sadat Khan and His Officers*, 20, 22, 93, *93*; cat. no. 54

   *Royal Lovers (A Prince Offering Wine to his Mistress)*, 20, 22, 92, *92*, 98; cat. no. 53

Delhi-Agra area:

   *Brahma Prostrates Himself Before Krishna* (*Bhagavata Purana*), 7, 28, *28*, 30; cat. no. 3

   *Nanda and Vasudeva* (*Bhagavata Purana*), 7, 27, *27*, 28, 30; cat. no. 2

Delhi-Agra area (probably):

   *The Gopis Beseech Krishna to Return Their Clothing* (Isarda *Bhagavata Purana*), 7, 27, 30, *30*; cat. no. 5

*Krishna Battles the Armies of the Demon Naraka* (*Bhagavata Purana*), 7, *8*, 29, *29*, 30, 38; cat. no. 4; fig. 4

*Krishna Kills the Evil King Kamsa's Washerman* (Isarda *Bhagavata Purana*), 7, 27, 31, *31*; cat. no. 6

Devgarh, 23, 125. *See also* Mewar or Devgarh

Devi, 18–19, 52, *52*, 70, 71, 72, *72*

Devidasa of Nurpur, *Shiva and Parvati Playing Chaupar* (*Rasamanjari*), 19, 76, 77, *77*; cat. no. 43

Devidasa of Nurpur (?), *King Dasharatha and His Royal Retinue Proceed to Rama's Wedding* (Shangri *Ramayana*), 19, 76, *76*; cat. no. 42

Dilaram, 39, *39*

Early Basohli Master, 74, 77

Early Basohli Master (attrib.):

   *Mudita Parakiya Nayika* (*Rasamanjari*), 19, 73, *73*, 74; cat. no. 39

   *The Worship of the Devi as the Dark Goddess Bhai Bhadrakali* (Tantric Devi series), 18, 72, *72*, 73, 74, 77; cat. no. 38

Early Mandi Master (attrib.), *A Marriage Procession in a Bazaar*, 10, 47, *47*; cat. no. 19

Farrukh Shah, 20, 21

Fatehpur Sikri, 9

Garuda, 29, *29*

Genghis Khan, 9

*Gita Govinda* (Song of the herdsman), 7, 22, 100, 104, *104*, 105, *105*; cat. nos. 63, 64

Golconda, 15, 17, 63

gopis, 30, *30*, 114, *114–15*. *See also* Rasalila

Gordhar, 94

Govardhan, 12

   *Akbar, with Lion and Heifer* (leaf from album for Shah Jahan), 14, 49, 51; cat. no. 22

Gujarat, 11

Guler (Punjab Hills), 19, 21, 22

   *Blindman's Bluff* (Manaku of Guler), 21, 100, *100–101*; cat. no. 60

   *Rama, Surrounded by the Armies of the Great Bear and Monkey Clans, Pardons Two Demon Spies* (Siege of Lanka series) (attrib. Manaku of Guler), 19, 21, 80, *80–81*, 82; cat. no. 46

*Rama and Lakshmana Overwhelmed by Arrows* (Siege of Lanka series) (attrib. Manaku of Guler), 19, 21, 82, *82–83*; cat. no. 47

Gupta period, 4–6

Hamid Bhakari, 40, *40–41*

Hamza, Prince, 32

*Hamza-nama* (Story of Prince Hamza), 9–10, 32, *33*, 34, *34*, *35*; cat. nos. 7, 8

*Harivamsa* (Genealogy of Vasudeva Krishna), 38, *38*; cat. no. 11

*Hasht Behesht* (Eight Paradises) of Amir Khosrow Dihlavi, 10, 39, *39*; cat. no. 12

Hermitage of Bharadvaja, 103, *103*

Hinduism, 3–4, 7–8

Hindu manuscripts, illustrated, 4–7, 15–16, 17

Hindu paintings. *See* Rajput (Hindu) style

Humayun, 9

Hunhar (attrib.), *Aurangzeb with His Third Son, Sultan Azam*, 14, 57, *57*; cat. no. 27

Hyderabad, 17

India, map of, 16th–19th c., 5; fig. 2

Indian music, 42

Iraj, 34, *34–35*

Isarda, 30. *See also Bhagavata Purana*, Isarda manuscript

Islam, 32. *See also* Mughal culture; Muslims

Jagat Singh, Maharaja, of Jaipur, 127

Jagat Singh, Maharana, 52

Jagat Singh, Maharana, of Mewar, 90, *90–91*

Jagat Singh I, Rao, 59, *59*, 61

Jagdish and Kamla Mittal Museum of Indian Art (Hyderabad), 123

Jagniwas Water Palace, 2, 22, 116, *116–17*

Jahangir (Salim), 12–13, 48, 49, 52, 53, 58. *See also* Mughal style, Jahangir period

Jainism, 6

Jain style, 7, 26

   *The Fourteen Auspicious Dreams of The Jina's Mother* (Kalpa Sutra), 6, 26, *26*; cat. no. 1

Jaipur (Rajasthan), 23, 124

   *The City and Hill Fortress of Ranthambhor*, 126–27, 127; cat. no. 79

   *Head of Krishna* (cartoon for mural of Rasalila) (attrib. Sahib Ram), 22, 119, *121*; cat. no. 75

   *Krishna and the Gopis Take Shelter from the Rain*, 22, 114, *114*, *115*; cat. no. 71

*Singer and Sarangi Player* (cartoon for mural of Rasalila) (attrib. Sahib Ram), 22, 119, *120*; cat. no. 74

Jaipur (?), *Tantric Form of Parama Shiva*, 133, *133*; cat. no. 83

Jai Singh of Amber, 106

Jai Singh II of Jaipur, 119

Jammu, 22. *See also* Bahu

Jasrota (Punjab Hills), 21

*Raja Balwant Singh of Jasrota Does Homage to Krishna and Radha* (attrib. Nainsukh of Guler), 22, 98, *98*; cat. no. 58

Jaunpur (Uttar Pradesh), *The Fourteen Auspicious Dreams of The Jina's Mother* (*Kalpa Sutra*), 6, 26, *26*; cat. no. 1

Jhilai (Rajasthan), 23, 124

*A Prince Hunting Boars with His Retinue*, 23, 124, *124*; cat. no. 77

Jodhpur, maharaja of, 123

Jwala, 72, *72*

Kali (goddess), 78

Kalis (emanations), 72, *72*

*Kalpa Sutra* (Book of rituals), 6, 26, *26*; cat. no. 1

Kamal Muhammad and Chand Muhammad, *The House of Bijapur*, 15, 68, *69*; cat. no. 36

Kangra (Punjab Hills), 22

*Krishna Woos Radha* (*Gita Govinda*), 22, 100, 105, *105*; cat. no. 64

*Radha Pining in the Wilderness* (*Gita Govinda*), 22, 100, 104, *104*, 105; cat. no. 63

*Rama, Sita, and Lakshmana at the Hermitage of Bharadvaja* (*Ramayana*), 20, 22, 100, 103, *103*; cat. no. 62; fig. 8

*The Village Beauty* (*Bihari Sat Sai*), 22, 100, 106, *106*; cat. no. 65

Kangra or Basohli, *The Marital Bliss of Nala and Damayanti* (*Nala-Damayanti*), 107, *107*; cat. no. 66

Karan Singh of Bikaner, 17, 46

Kedar Ragini, 65, *65*

Khambhavati Ragini, 42

Khemkaran, *Prince Riding on an Elephant*, 36, *36*, 45; cat. no. 9

Khurram, Prince (Shah Jahan), 49, *50*, 58. *See also* Shah Jahan

Kishangarh (Rajasthan), 21, 94, 95, 96, 113

*Krishna and Radha Lie in a Bower* (attrib. Nihal Chand), 21, 22, 96, 113, *113*; cat. no. 70

*A Lady Playing the Tanpura*, 21, 96, *97*; cat. no. 57

*Laila and Majnun Converse Beneath a Tree* (Nihal Chand), 21, 95, *95*; cat. no. 56

*Prince Padam Singh of Bikaner with his Bard, Gordhar, on a Terrace at Night* (attrib. Bhavani Das), 21, 94, *94*; cat. no. 55

Koran, 3

Kota (Rajasthan), 15, 17–18, 23, 45, 61, 123

*The Marriage Celebrations at Udaipur of Maharao Ram Singh II of Kota*, 128, *128*, 129; cat. no. 80

*Rao Bhoj Singh of Bundi Slays a Lion* (attrib. Kota Master), 62–63, *63*; cat. no. 31

*Rao Jagat Singh I in His Garden* (Kota Master), 18, 59, *59*; cat. no. 29

*A Tiger Hunt* (Sheikh Taju), 22, *122–23*, 123; cat. no. 76

*Two Elephants Fighting* (Kota Master), 18, *60–61*, 61; cat. no. 30

Kota Master, 63

*Rao Jagat Singh I in His Garden*, 18, 59, *59*; cat. no. 29

*Two Elephants Fighting*, 18, *60–61*, 61; cat. no. 30

Kota Master (attrib.), *Rao Bhoj Singh of Bundi Slays a Lion*, 62–63, *63*; cat. no. 31

Kripal Pal, Maharaja, 74, 76

Krishna, 3, 7, 21, 27, 28, *28*, 29, *29*, 30, *30*, 31, *31*, 38, *38*, 43, *43*, 73, 78, 84, *85*, *85*, 98, *98*, 99, *99*, 100, *100–101*, 102, *102*, 104, *104*, 105, *105*, 106, 113, *113*, 114, *114*, 119, *121*. *See also* Rasalila

Kundalini yoga, 133

Lahore, 10, 12

*Bahram Gur Watching Dilaram Charm the Wild Animals With Her Music* (*Hasht Behesht*) (attrib. Miskin), 10, 39, *39*; cat. no. 12

*Hamid Bhakari Punished by Akbar* (*Akbar-nama*) (attrib. Manohar), 10, 40, *40–41*; cat. no. 13

*Krishna and Balarama Fight the Enemy* (*Harivamsa*), 38, *38*; cat. no. 11

Laila, 95, *95*

Lakshmana, 82, *82–83*, 103, *103*

Lodi Sultan of Delhi, 9

Madhu Singh, Raja, 18

Mahadeva (Shiva), 72

Majnun, 95, *95*

Malwa (Rajasthan), 11

*Ragini Kakubha* (*Ragamala* series), 11, 44, *44*; cat. no. 16

Manaku of Guler, 21, 22, 80, 82, 100

*Blindman's Bluff*, 21, 100, *100*, *101*; cat. no. 60

Manaku of Guler (attrib.):

*Rama, Surrounded by the Armies of the Great Bear and Monkey Clans, Pardons Two Demon Spies* (Siege of Lanka series), 19, 21, 80, *80–81*, 82; cat. no. 46

*Rama and Lakshmana Overwhelmed by Arrows* (Siege of Lanka series), 19, 21, 82, *82–83*; cat. no. 47

Mandi (Punjab Hills), 10, 78

*The Goddess Kali Slaying Demons* (attrib. Mandi Master), 78, *78*; cat. no. 44

*Maharaja Sidh Sen Receiving an Embassy* (Mandi Master), 78–79, *79*; cat. no. 45

*A Marriage Procession in a Bazaar* (attrib. Early Mandi Master), 10, 47, *47*; cat. no. 19

Mandi Master, 78

*Maharaja Sidh Sen Receiving an Embassy*, 78–79, *79*; cat. no. 45

Mandi Master (attrib.), *The Goddess Kali Slaying Demons*, 78, *78*; cat. no. 44

Mankot (Punjab Hills), 19, 84

*The Demon Pralamba Carries Off Balarama* (*Bhagavata Purana*), 19, 84, *84*, 102; cat. no. 48

Manohar, 12

Manohar (attrib.), *Hamid Bhakari Punished by Akbar* (*Akbar-nama*), 10, 40, *40*, 41; cat. no. 13

Mansur, 48

*Nilgai (Blue Bull)* (leaf from album for Shah Jahan), 12, 48, *48*; cat. no. 20

Marwar, 14

Mathura, 14

Mesbah, 32, *33*

Mewar (Rajasthan), 11, 19–20, 23, 90, 116, 125

*Khambhavati Ragini* (Chawand *Ragamala* series) (Nasir ud-Din), 11, 42, *42*, 44; cat. no. 14

*Maharana Amar Singh II, Prince Sangram Singh, and Courtiers Watch the Performance of an Acrobat and Musicians*, 20, 88, *88–89*; cat. no. 51

*Maharana Ari Singh with His Courtiers at the Jagniwas Water Palace* (Bhima, Kesu Ram, Bhopa, Nathu), 2, 22, 116, *116–17*; cat. no. 72; fig. 1

*Maharana Jagat Singh of Mewar Hawking for Cranes* (Shiva and Dayal), 20, 90, *90–91*; cat. no. 52
*Shah Jahan Hunting Deer with Trained Cheetahs*, 20, 86, *86, 87*; cat. no. 50
Mewar or Devgarh, *Maharana Bhim Singh of Mewar and His Retinue Going to a Hunt* (attrib. Chokha), 23, 125, *125*; cat. no. 78
Mir Sayyid Ali, 9
*Bahram Gur Pins the Coupling Onagers* (*Shah-nama*), 9, 11; fig. 5
Mirza Ubed Beg, 18
Miskin, 39
Miskin (attrib.), *Bahram Gur Watching Dilaram Charm the Wild Animals With Her Music* (*Hasht Behesht*), 10, 39, *39*; cat. no. 12
Mount Govardhan, 114
Mount Kailasa, 133
Mudita Parakiya Nayika, 73, *73*
Mughal (Muslim) culture, 3, 4, 9–17, 18, 19, 20–23, 30, 45, 47, 58, 61, 64, 68, 79, 86, 88, 94, 96, 99, 112, 119
Mughal style:
   Akbar period
      *Assad Ibn Kariba Attacks the Army of Iraj Suddenly by Night* (*Hamza-nama*), 9, 34, *34–35*; cat. no. 8
      *Bahram Gur Watching Dilaram Charm the Wild Animals With Her Music* (*Hasht Behesht*) (attrib. Miskin), 10, 39, *39*; cat. no. 12
      *Hamid Bhakari Punished by Akbar* (*Akbar-nama*) (attrib. Manohar), 10, 40, *40–41*; cat. no. 13
      *Krishna and Balarama Fight the Enemy* (*Harivamsa*), 38, *38*; cat. no. 11
      *Mesbah the Grocer Brings the Spy Parran to His House* (*Hamza-nama*), 9, 32, *33*; cat. no. 7
      *Prince Riding on an Elephant* (Khemkaran), 36, *36*, 45; cat. no. 9
      *Royal Riding Horse and Runner*, 37, *37*, 45; cat. no. 10
   Aurangzeb period, *Aurangzeb with His Third Son, Sultan Azam* (attrib. Hunhar), 14, 57, *57*; cat. no. 27
   Jahangir period
      *Nilgai (Blue Bull)* (leaf from album for Shah Jahan) (Mansur), 12, 48, *48*; cat. no. 20

*Prince Khurram (Shah Jahan) with His Son Dara Shikoh* (leaf from album for Shah Jahan) (Nanha), 12, 49, *50*; cat. no. 21
   Muhammad Shah period
      *Muhammad Shah Enthroned with Sadat Khan and His Officers*, 20, 22, 93, *93*; cat. no. 54
      *Royal Lovers (A Prince Offering Wine to his Mistress)*, 20, 22, 92, *92*, 98; cat. no. 53
   Shah Jahan period
      *Akbar, with Lion and Heifer* (leaf from album for Shah Jahan) (Govardhan), 14, 49, *51*; cat. no. 22
      *Shah Jahan on a Terrace Holding a Pendant Set with His Portrait* (leaf from album for Shah Jahan) (Chitarman), 13, *13*, 14, 53, *54*; cat. no. 24; fig. 6
      *Shah Jahan Watching an Elephant Fight* (*Padshah-nama*) (Bulaqi), 14, 53, 55, 61; cat. no. 25
      *Shamsa (Rosette) Bearing the Name and Titles of the Emperor Shah Jahan* (leaf from album for Shah Jahan), 14, 53, *56*; cat. no. 26
      *Shri Bhairavi Devi* (attrib. Payag), 14, 52, *52*; cat. no. 23
Muhammad Amir of Karraya, Shayk, *A Syce Holding Two Carriage Horses*, 130, *130–31*; cat. no. 81
Muhammad Shah, 20, 21, 22, 93, *93*, 104, 109. *See also* Mughal style, Muhammad Shah period
Muslims, 3–4, 7, 14, 32, 66. *See also* Mughal (Muslim) culture

Nader Shah, 20, 22
Nagari Das, Maharaja, of Kishangarh, 113
Nainsukh of Guler, 21–22, 98, 99
Nainsukh of Guler (attrib.):
   *Krishna Steals the Butter*, 22, 99, *99*; cat. no. 59
   *Raja Balwant Singh of Jasrota Does Homage to Krishna and Radha*, 22, 98, *98*; cat. no. 58
Nala, 107, *107*
*Nala-Damayanti (Romance of Nala and Damayanti)*, 107, *107*; cat. no. 66
Nanda, 27, *27*
Nanha, *Prince Khurram (Shah Jahan) with His Son Dara Shikoh* (leaf from album for Shah Jahan), 12, 49, *50*; cat. no. 21

Naraka, 29, *29*
Nasir ud-Din, *Khambhavati Ragini* (Chawand *Ragamala* series), 11, 42, *42*, 44; cat. no. 14
Nihal Chand, 21, 95
   *Laila and Majnun Converse Beneath a Tree*, 21, 95, *95*; cat. no. 56
Nihal Chand (attrib.), *Krishna and Radha Lie in a Bower*, 21, 22, 96, 113, *113*; cat. no. 70

Oudh (Uttar Pradesh), *A Holi Celebration*, 22, *108–9*, 109; cat. no. 67

Padam Singh, Prince, of Bikaner, 94, *94*
*Padshah-nama* (History of the emperor), 13, 14, 53, 55, 61; cat. no. 25
Pahari painting. *See* Punjab Hills
*Pancavimsatisahasrika Prajnaparamita*, 6, *6*; fig. 3
Panchama Ragini, 46, *46*
Parama Shiva, 133, *133*
Parran, 32, *33*
Parvati, 77, *77*
Payag (attrib.), *Shri Bhairavi Devi*, 14, 52, *52*; cat. no. 23
Peacock Throne (of Shah Jahan), 20
Persia, 7, 15, 66, 112
   Tabriz, *Bahram Gur Pins the Coupling Onagers* (Mir Sayyid Ali), 9, *11*; fig. 5
Persian style, 12, 32, 34, 36, 37, 39
Pralamba, 84, *84*
Punjab Hills, 3, 15, 18–19, 21, 22, 23, 74, 80, 92, 93. *See also* Bahu; Basohli; Guler; Jasrota; Kangra; Mandi; Mankot

Radha, 3, 21, 98, *98*, 104, *104*, 105, *105*, 113, *113*, 114, *114–15*, 119
*Ragamala* series (Garland of musical modes), 7, 11, 12, 17, 44, *44*, 46, *46*, 47, 65, *65*; cat. nos. 16, 18, 33
   Chawand version, 11, 42, *42*, 44; cat. no. 14
Raghugarh, 11–12
Ragini Kakubha, 44, *44*
Rajasthan, 23. *See also* Amber; Bikaner; Bundi; Jaipur; Jhilai; Kishangarh; Kota; Malwa; Mewar
Rajasthani kingdoms, 3, 4, 10–12, 14, 15–21, 22
Rajasthani style, 92, 93, 96, 116
Rajput (Hindu) kingdoms, 3, 4, 23

Rajput (Hindu) style, 7–8, 9, 10–12, 18, 19–20, 22, 27, 42, 42, 45, 49, 50, 73, 73, 79, 86, 88, 99, 99, 112, 112, 113, 125. *See also* Chaurapanchasika style
Raktabija, 72
Rama, 74, 75, 80, 80, 82, 82–83, 103, 103
*Ramayana* (Story of King Rama), 20, 22, 47, 80, 100, 103, 103; cat. no. 62; fig. 8
Shangri version, 19, 74, 75, 76, 76, 84; cat. nos. 40, 41, 42
Ram Singh II, Maharao, of Kota, 128, 128–29
Ranthambhor Fortress, 126–27, 127
Rasalila (Circle dance of Krishna and the *gopis*), cartoon for mural of, 22, 119, 120, 121; cat. nos. 74, 75
*Rasamanjari* (Essence of the experience of delight), 7, 19, 73, 73, 74, 76, 77, 77; cat. nos. 39, 43
*Rasikapriya* (Garden of delights), 7
Boston manuscript, 12, 43, 43; cat. no. 15
Raton, Rao, of Bundi, 58, 58
Ravana, 80
Ruknuddin, 17, 64, 65
*Kedar Ragini* (*Ragamala* series), 17, 65, 65; cat. no. 33
*Ladies on a Terrace*, 15, 16, 17, 64, 64, 65; cat. no. 32; fig. 7

Sadat Khan, 93
Sahib Ram, 119

Sahib Ram (attrib.):
*Head of Krishna* (cartoon for mural of Rasalila), 22, 119, 121; cat. no. 75
*Singer and Sarangi Player* (cartoon for mural of Rasalila), 22, 119, 120; cat. no. 74
Salim. *See* Jahangir
Sangram Pal, Raja, 18, 19
Sangram Singh, 88, 88–89
Sansar Chand, 22
Sardar Singh, Maharaja, of Bikaner, 132–33, 132
Sati, 72
*Sat Sai*, 106
Savant Singh, Raja, 21
Sawai Pratap Singh, Maharaja, 119
Sesha, 102, 102
Shah Jahan, 13–14, 13, 17, 18, 49, 50, 52, 53, 54, 55, 64, 86, 86. *See also* Mughal style, Shah Jahan period
*Shah-nama* (Book of kings) (Shah Tahmasp), 9, 11; fig. 5
Shah Tahmasp, 9, 11
*Shah-nama* (Book of kings), 9, 11; fig. 5
Shakti, 133
Shangri Style I Master, 84
Shangri Style I Master (attrib.):
*Rama Visits His Mother Before His Exile* (Shangri *Ramayana*), 19, 74, 75, 84; cat. no. 40
*The Sage Vasishta Visits Rama* (Shangri *Ramayana*), 19, 74, 75, 84; cat. no. 41
Shangri Style II Master, 76

Sheikh Taju, 123
*A Tiger Hunt*, 22, 122–23, 123; cat. no. 76
Sher Shah, 9
Shiva, 52, 65, 71, 77, 77, 78, 133
Shiva and Dayal, *Maharana Jagat Singh of Mewar Hawking for Cranes*, 90, 90–91; cat. no. 52
Shri Bhairavi Devi, 52, 52
Sidh Sen, Maharaja, 78–79, 79
Siege of Lanka series, 19, 21, 80, 80–81, 82, 82–83; cat. nos. 46, 47
Sita, 74, 75, 103, 103
Sufis, 68

Tabriz (Persia), 9
Tamerlane, 9
Tantric Devi series, 18, 72, 72, 73, 74, 77; cat. no. 38
Turkestan, 7
Turkey, 15
Turkoman, 63

Uttar Pradesh. *See* Jaunpur; Oudh

Vasishta, 74, 75
Vasudeva, 27, 27
Vishnu, 74, 102, 102

Zayn-al-din, *A Cheetah*, 23, 109, 110–11; cat. no. 60

# PHOTOGRAPH CREDITS